PASTRY
· MAGIC ·

PASTRY
·MAGIC·

Carol Pastor

CASSELL

To Terry, Maxwell, Ron and Eileen

A CASSELL BOOK

First published in the UK 1993 by
Cassell, Villiers House, 41/47 Strand, London WC2N 5JE

Distributed in Australia by Capricorn Link (Australia) Pty Ltd
P.O. Box 665, Lane Cove, NSW 2066

British Library Cataloguing-in-Publication Data
A catalogue record for this book is available from the British Library

ISBN 0-304-34239-4

Typeset by MS Filmsetting Limited, Frome, Somerset

Printed in Slovenia by printing house Mladinska Knjiga
by arrangement with Korotan Italiana, Ljubljana

Jacket: Autumn Tartlets (see page 70)

CONTENTS

THE HISTORY OF PASTRY AND PIE MAKING

In its earliest form English pastry was a rather heavy, solid affair, regarded more as a means of enclosing food and keeping in the juices and aroma while it was baking. The pastry cases were originally called coffers, and they were made of huff paste, a close, unleavened mixture of crude flour and water. Coffers were not intended to be eaten, and they were probably based on the Roman custom of cooking food while it was sealed inside a paste shell of flour and oil.

These 'standing pies' gradually went out of favour, and pies and tarts came to be prepared in patty pans made of shorter, more flavoursome and edible pastry. This pastry, which was made of flour, fat and milk and sometimes ale, required less cooking time than the disposable crust of the standing pie.

By the seventeenth century a really rich paste of flour, butter, eggs, rosewater and spices was in use. It was made by daubing butter on paste, folding the paste over the butter and rolling it out again, then repeating the process five or six times more. This was known as puff pastry, and it is said to have been discovered by the Frenchman Claude Gelée, who is better known as Claude Lorraine (1600-82), the landscape painter and draughtsman. Legend recounts how, in his absent-minded youth as a baker's apprentice, Gelée once forgot to add butter to the dough and, in his attempts to remedy the oversight as quickly as he could, wrapped the butter in the dough. The resulting pastry was tender, airy and puffy – and tasted extremely good. A more likely but less appealing explanation is that the idea of puff pastry was brought to Europe much earlier by the Crusaders. It is said that the French tried to keep the method secret but that it was spread by word of mouth.

Another pastry that originated in France was *crocant* or crackling paste, a thin, crisp crust made of flour, sugar and egg white that was cut into rounds and used as a base or top cover for fruit confections.

The origins of the word pie are still unclear. It has been suggested that it derives from magpie – just as the bird is a collector of different objects, so a pie conceals an assortment of ingredients.

In Tudor and Stuart England pies were spectacular and frivolous set-pieces at banquets, although they were not always filled with edible victuals. Robert May, a noted seventeenth-century cookery writer, gives an informative account of such a banquet. He tells of a giant gilded pastry stag, from which a bread arrow was plucked and which bled claret all over the fine damask tablecloth. He writes, too, of a castle made with unbelievable intricacy – the battlements, portcullises and drawbridge were made of pasteboard, gilded with bay leaves. The castle opened fire on a pasteboard ship at the other end of the table, the guns 'going off like crackers, leaving such an acrid smell of gunpowder in the great hall that ... ladies sweetened the stink by breaking eggshells containing sweet water and threw them at each other'.

In the early sixteenth century some pies were made with coarse paste and coloured yellow with saffron or egg yolks – out of them emerged live birds or frogs. One of the best known of these creations is remembered in the nursery rhyme *Four and Twenty Blackbirds*. Who or what these birds were meant to represent has been the subject of endless debate. It has been suggested that they were the choirs of the monasteries about to be dissolved by Henry VIII. A sinister explanation of the maid whose nose is pecked off is that she was the unfortunate Anne Boleyn. Another theory is that the blackbirds represent the letters of the alphabet (although why there should be 24 rather than 26 is unclear) and that the rhyme celebrates the first printing in English in 1535 of the Bible. Choirs, letters or politicians? A more probable explanation is that the pie was simply an amusing entertainment for dinner guests.

The live contents of pies were not always small animals and birds. Children, acrobats and singing dwarfs also appeared from time to time. Jeffrey Hudson (1619-82), the dwarf of the Duke of Buckingham, was served at table in a cold pasty out of which he briskly emerged, brandishing a sword and saluting Charles I and his queen Henrietta Maria, in whose honour the banquet was being held and to whom the dwarf was given as a page.

These novel centre-pieces were ingeniously contrived. The covered pastry shell was baked blind with a temporary filling of bran. When the pie was cooked the bran was removed and the cargo inserted through a hole in the bottom crust, which was sealed with more paste.

In the sixteenth and seventeenth centuries sweet tarts often contained flower petals, such as marigold and cowslip, which were chopped into small pieces and combined with sweet biscuits, rosewater, cream, eggs and spices to make rich, yellow cream fillings. Other tarts sometimes contained puréed syrupy confections of ruby red rosehips, roses and quinces, medlars and green plums, which were pounded to a pulp or puréed through a hair sieve. The fruit 'tartstuff' was rarely cooked in pieces as we would prepare an apple pie today because of a general mistrust of uncooked fruit, which was often blamed for sudden fevers, rashes and uncommon illnesses.

Savoury fillings included puréed peas, savoury sorrel or spinach. The lids were sweet or savoury, regardless of the contents of the pie. Even pies including meat or fish were iced with sugar. A spectacular medieval 'fysshe tart' is known to have been layered with a rich black and white filling of figs, prunes and almonds alternating with white fish and currants, the whole laced with pungent spices and extravagantly gilded with gold leaf and finished off with a fish tail coming out of the hole in the top.

At Christmas minced pies or 'shred pies' containing shredded meat, dried fruits and seasoning were made in rectangular, cradle-shaped tins. The crust or coffin represented the manger of the Nativity story, and the savoury ingredients embodied the gifts of spices brought by the Three Kings. It was not until the eighteenth century that a distinction began to be made between savoury and sweet pies, and the meat came to be omitted, leaving just the dried fruit, spices and suet, although the name, minced meat (later, mincemeat), was retained.

By the late eighteenth century cooks had a wide repertoire of pastries. Mrs De Salis's pastry book, which dates from 1772, lists many that are unfamiliar to us today – orange-flavoured pastry, royal pastry, which was more like choux, Spanish pastry, which was made from hog's fat, flour and butter, and rice pastry, which was made with boiled, pounded rice, flour and eggs – and that were made for a variety of fillings. A Yorkshire recipe dating from 1765 for a Christmas pie tells us to make

a standing crust from one peck of flour and six pounds of butter boiled in a gallon of water. Skim off the butter into the flour with as little liquor as you can, work it well up into a paste and pull it into pieces when it is cold, then make it into a thick standing crust. Then fill it with a turkey, a goose, a fowl, a partridge and a pigeon, boned by opening down the back and highly seasoned, covering one with the other so that the last looks like one large turkey. Then fill the corners with a hare and woodcock cut into small pieces.

A huge quantity of butter was pressed over the top of the meat, which was covered with a thick lid of paste before being cooked for four hours. The whole dish was sent to London in a Christmas box.

One of the greatest pastry cooks of the nineteenth century was Antonin Carême (1783-1883), an artistic genius, whose pastry creations were often based on architectural drawings. He is credited with the invention of the croquembouche, the mille-feuille and the vol-au-vent and with having perfected puff pastry. He cooked for the Prince Regent, later George IV (1762-1830), for £1,000 a year in the extravagant, simulated palm-tree pillared kitchens of the Royal Pavilion in Brighton. He returned to France after only a year because of home-sickness and because of a great dislike of English fog.

In Victorian times the cooks in large town and country houses would rise at the crack of dawn to make pastry while the kitchen was still cool. In the country they made gigantic pies to feed the shooting parties, while for grand functions they created exquisitely made pies, with ornately gilded crusts covered in intricate patterns of oak leaves, acorns, rose leaves and rosettes. The rich, hot fillings were lobster, or mutton and turnips, or veal and olives. For many years pigeon pies were served with four cleaned pigeons' feet encrusted in the pastry lid to show what the pie contained, a custom designated as objection-able and useless in 1877 in Kettner's *Book of the Table*.

Mrs Beeton wrote wonderful recipes for pies, some of which were refined, although others seem rather bizarre. The revised edition of *Household Management*, which appeared in 1906, included a recipe for parrot pie that used a dozen parakeets.

As numbers of household staff fell and kitchens became smaller, the passion for very rich, ornate pies seems to have declined. An early labour-saving device was the lidded casserole dish, sometimes made in pale cream biscuit-ware in imitation of a raised pie crust, and this quickly came to be used to save the time that had been spent in making pie crusts.

In Britain during World War II rationing reduced pastries to butter-less and egg-less versions of the rich crusts of earlier times. The government issued advice on how to produce yet more economical pastries, requiring a bare minimum of fat and using oatmeal in place of flour. One recipe used potatoes to lighten the flour, and potato pastry became the standard topping for Woolton Pie, a vegetable dish whose ingredients could be changed according to availability and which was named after Lord Woolton, the Minister of Food (1940-43), who had introduced rationing to wartime Britain with the challenge that all should 'make do and use food wisely'.

More recently, travel and experience of different culinary traditions have widened the range of pastries available to us and made us more aware of the varieties that are on offer, although vacuum-packed pies will never quite match the culinary heights known to our ancestors.

THE PASTRIES USED IN THIS BOOK

The art of good pastry making often lies more in the execution than in the ingredients. A cool, quick and light touch and an instinctive feel for when the texture of the dough is right come from patience and experience, and from a desire to make melt-in-the-mouth pastry as the foundation of many delicious dishes and as a wonderful contrast to the flavours of the fillings. There are many different pastries to choose from, and some of these can be bought ready-made and frozen from supermarkets. With few exceptions, however, the best pastries come from our own kitchens, where they can be made from fine, pure and fresh ingredients and eaten warm, straight from the oven.

SHORTCRUST

This deliciously short, crumbly pastry and its variations is probably the best known and most commonly used. Used for baked tarts of fruit or jam or as the basis of savoury flans, shortcrust pastry is one of the essential ingredients of the quintessential English afternoon tea.

Perfect shortcrust pastry requires a delicate hand and cool fingertips to rub in the ingredients. A light touch is essential. Heavy kneading or over-handling the dough will develop the protein-forming gluten in the flour and make it more elastic so that the pastry is hard and heavy. Gluten is present in all types of flour, but especially in the strong flours used for bread making, when heavy kneading is necessary to promote elasticity and make a stronger dough.

Another tip is to bind the ingredients with carefully measured quantities of egg and water to make a moist, soft dough. Too much liquid will make a hard pastry that will shrink during cooking; too little liquid will make a dough that is difficult to handle and that will crack when it is rolled out. It is also essential to observe the chilling periods to eliminate shrinkage, which can cause the pastry to look misshapen.

There are two types of shortcrust – a plain pastry that has no eggs and a rich version, which includes a larger proportion of butter and uses an egg yolk mixed with water. A mixture of fats gives the best results. Use butter for flavour, colour and texture, and fat (lard) to make the pastry light (or short). Crushed nuts, grated cheese and other flavourings can be added to vary the basic recipe.

PUFF PASTRY

Air and moisture are captured in the pastry between each rolling and folding of the oblong-shaped dough, which is turned to the right each time to form a 3-layered, open-sided slab. This process – the turn – is repeated six times to make a rich, buttery dough composed of thin layers, which will, during cooking, rise to make a smooth, richly golden and fully puffed crust with a delicious fragrance of butter.

The preparation of puff pastry is lengthy, and it is said to be the hardest pastry to make, although with patience it can be mastered. The most important aspect, apart from observing the chilling periods and keeping an accurate count of the turns, is to prepare it in a cool kitchen with chilled ingredients, including iced water. The whole operation will be ruined if the butter becomes too soft. Even professional cooks have been driven to despair at the sight of sticky butter oozing through the layers of pastry or a spiritless mass of crust caused by lack of turning. Antonin Carême is said to have remarked that the 'summer makes our operations difficult and laborious, especially puff pastry, which cannot be done well without cooling it on ice, which then renders it as firm as in the month of January'.

FLAKY PASTRY

This is formed of thin, crisp layers. It is similar to puff pastry and is cooked at the same temperature, but is not as light and has fewer layers. Flaky pastry is suitable for pastries that are to be served cold such as sausage rolls and meat pasties and some sweet pastries. It is made by folding and rolling dough into layers and daubing fat in between. The pieces of fat cause air pockets to form, and these help to separate the flakes.

HOT WATER CRUST

This pastry is similar to those early crusts that were simply pastes to enclose and protect meat during cooking and that were often discarded afterwards. It is a hard, plain, rather bland-tasting pastry, which is stiff enough to be raised – that is, it will stand alone, unsupported by a dish. It is often made in hinged moulds or pressed around wooden pie moulds to hold substantial fillings of meat, game or poultry. Unlike other pastries, it must be kept warm while it is made. If the lard is allowed to set the pastry becomes cracked and unmanageable. Hot water crust holds its shape well during cooking and is ideal for creating intricate decorations of crescents and diamonds in the French style or roses and leaves. It is traditionally used to make the handsome game pies that are served at cold buffets.

WHOLEMEAL PASTRY

Many vegetarian dishes use wholemeal pastry, which has a nutty flavour and a good texture, making it a useful complement to tenderly cooked vegetables and fruit, which themselves may have little texture. Wholemeal pastry using all wholemeal flour is a little heavy for my taste, and I mix equal parts of white and wholemeal flour to lighten it while retaining the pastry's characteristic delicious taste and wholesome texture.

FILO PASTRY

The name filo or phyllo derives from the Greek word for leaf, and the pastry itself is paper-thin. In Austria, where it is known as strudel pastry, cooks say you should roll it so thin that you can read your love letters through it. Frozen filo pastry is available from most delicatessens and Greek speciality food stores and from some supermarkets, and it is sold ready-rolled in leaves. Although filo pastry can be made quite easily and quickly at home, the result will be no better than a bought pastry, mainly because it is so difficult to roll it out to the correct paper-thinness without tearing it. This crisply textured pastry is ideal for strudels – apple being the best known – but it is equally delicious filled with cream cheese and served with hot cherry sauce. It is also used for tartlets and canapés filled with soft cheeses and fruits that need little cooking.

HERB PASTRY

A variation of shortcrust, herb pastry is an unusual alternative for savoury pies and flans.

PÂTÉ SUCRÉE

This rich, crisp and textured sweet pastry, which is also known as French flan pastry or biscuit pastry, is used mostly for sweet tarts. It is generally lightly flavoured with vanilla or sometimes orange zest or ground almonds. The paste is made in a different way from shortcrust – pâté sucrée is worked with quick movements of the fingertips. It is firm and inelastic, and it keeps its shape during cooking, which makes it an ideal pastry for intricate decorations and mouldings. Motifs of flowers and leaves made from pâté sucrée are often used to decorate open fruit tarts and tartlets.

It should be cooked until it is biscuit coloured. Never over-cook it or leave it in the oven once the edge of the pastry has started to brown. The high sugar content means that it burns quickly, and over-cooked pâté sucrée can taste slightly bitter.

PÂTÉ BRISÉE

The French equivalent of English shortcrust, pâté brisée is traditionally made in much the same way as pâté sucrée – that is, directly on a pastry board or marble slab – but it is less rich and unsweetened, and it has a rather plain taste and a hard, crunchy texture. Its redeeming features are that it can hold both sweet and savoury moist fillings for a long time without become soft and soggy. It is, therefore, a useful pastry for caterers and patissiers, who often use it as the base of open-faced tartlets and flans.

CHOUX PASTRY

In its uncooked state choux pastry is soft enough to be piped into small shapes, which puff and crisp lightly during cooking to double their size, conveniently leaving a cavity in the centre into which fillings of flavoured creams can be piped. Use it to make mouth-watering éclairs and other light confections. A group of *cygnes en pâté à choux* (cream puff swans), floating gracefully over a pool of fruit coulis or rich chocolate sauce, will make an elegant and feather-light finale to a meal. Another delicious dish to end a meal is Paris-Brest, a choux ring filled with praline cream and topped with almonds and a dusting of icing sugar, which was named after the nineteenth-century cycle race that took place over a circular route from Paris to Brest.

Small choux puffs are sometimes pressed together with a light, sticky caramel and built into a peak, which can be as much as 3 feet/1 metre high, to form a croquembouche, the standard *pièce montée* or table centre-piece of a French wedding. Choux pastry can also be used for savoury dishes such as gougère, for which gruyère cheese is added to the raw dough before it is piped around a mixture of ham, chicken and mushrooms.

MASCARPONE AND SOURED CREAM PASTRY

Mascarpone (or mascherpone) is a very creamy soft cheese from Italy, and it is used to make this mild-flavoured, tender and appetizing pastry. It is especially delicious with fruit fillings.

CREAM CHEESE PASTRY

This pastry is a firm favourite in the United States, partly because it is quick and easy to make. Surprisingly, the flavour is not overwhelmingly cheesy but is rather subtle and pleasing. The texture is smooth and light, and the pastry can be used for both sweet and savoury pies.

ORANGE AND CARDAMOM PASTRY

Pies and tarts containing acidic fruit are well suited to this warm and spicy sweet pastry. Try it at Christmas for cranberry pies and tartlets.

CHOCOLATE PASTRY

This useful variation on pâté sucrée makes ideal containers for fillings that have caramel, chocolate or vanilla flavours.

ACHIEVING A PROFESSIONAL FINISH

PASTRY BRUSHES

Decorative cooking is an art form, and, just as an artist has a jar overflowing with different brushes, so must the cook.

In 1845 Eliza Acton wrote in *Modern Cookery for Private Families* that a fine yellow glaze appropriate to a meat pie should be laid on with a paste brush or a small bunch of feathers. Today's innovative cook may not have a bunch of feathers but will undoubtedly have a selection of good brushes close to hand, ready to apply a wash of beaten egg to give a rich golden glaze to a baked pie or to paint warm jam glaze over each individual fruit in an open tart to make them glisten like bright jewels in a golden case.

Standard pastry brushes of hair or bristle can be bought from all kitchen hardware shops, but you will find a better selection in shops that supply artists' materials. Look out for good quality, fine brushes for your detailed work. Chinese gift shops often stock a range of white goat's hair brushes in a variety of sizes. These are cheap to buy and invaluable for egg-washing large areas of pastry, as long as you

don't mind rescuing the occasional fine hair that becomes dislodged from the brush. The smaller and softer decorators' brushes that are sold in hardware and do-it-yourself stores are ideal, and they are sometimes also available in kitchen hardware shops.

Incidentally, if you do live in the country, a small bunch of soft white chicken feathers, tied to the end of a pencil or piece of wooden dowelling for a handle, makes a splendid brush.

GLAZES AND EGG WASHES

In the Middle Ages cooks sometimes added brilliant colours to food, using eggs and saffron to make pastry a rich golden yellow. Fish pies were usually liberally coated in sugar and set in the oven to form a rich crust. A sixteenth-century recipe includes directions to strew sugar over the baked pie top and glaze it with a red-hot fire shovel.

We are still embellishing our pastry in much the same ways as the earliest pie-makers to make our pies look appealing and appetizing. Instead of fire shovels, today's cooks can use special catering glazing irons to add caramelized patterns to the lids of pastries topped with snowy white sugar. Egg washes and sugar glazes are used to give pastries and pies shiny golden finishes.

Hot Sugar and Butter

Melt equal quantities of sugar and butter; paint over pies 5 minutes before the end of cooking to give a clear, shiny finish. Use this glaze on filo pastries with sweet fillings; omit the sugar for savoury fillings.

Saffron Egg Wash

For a long time *Crocus sativus*, from which saffron comes, was grown mainly in the area around Saffron Walden in Essex in southern England. A tiny

amount of saffron added to egg glaze gives a rather special golden finish to pie crusts and pastry.

Add a good pinch of saffron strands to 1 tablespoon of hand-hot milk and leave to stand for 1 hour, until the milk has turned a bright yellow. Strain the milk and whisk it with the yolk of 1 egg and a pinch of salt.

Egg Glaze

Egg yolks themselves can vary widely in colour. Some are a pale, insipid lemon colour, others are a rich golden yellow, and this can make a difference to the richness of the glaze.

Add 1 egg yolk and a pinch of salt to 1 tablespoon of milk in a small bowl. Whisk well together and use to paint over pastry pies and the edges of open tarts to give a warm golden finish. To make a slightly richer glaze, add an extra egg yolk and a good pinch of salt and sugar.

Always paint egg glaze thinly to give a more even finish and to avoid drips. This is especially important when you are using it with puff pastry, because if the glaze drips over the sides of the pie or pastry decorations it will stick the delicate layers together and stop them puffing up. It is always better to glaze the individual decorations before you add them to the pie lid. A double coating of egg glaze will give a deeper golden colour; always chill the pastry well before you apply the second coat.

Whisked Egg White

Sweet pies were traditionally glazed with lightly beaten egg white and sugar. For best results, apply the glaze either before you put the pie in the oven or shortly before the end of baking, when you should remove the pie from the oven, lightly brush it with egg white, sprinkle over caster sugar and return the pie to the oven for 5-6 minutes.

Glazing with Icing Sugar

A lovely brittle, polished-looking finish can be achieved by sifting icing sugar lightly over the surface of freshly cooked pies and pastries and setting them under a hot grill until the sugar melts and caramelizes into a crisp glaze. Do keep a constant eye on pastries under the grill because it takes only a minute or so for the glaze to form and the sugar can burn very quickly. Don't worry about the odd scorched patch – these won't detract from the appearance of the pie or taste in any way.

Caramelizing with a Hot Iron

A hot glazing iron can be used to create interesting effects by caramelizing the surface of sugar-coated pastries. This technique is used by many chefs and caterers to decorate pastries such as mille-feuilles and tartlets containing pears, apples and apricots. The pastry is evenly coated with sifted icing sugar, which is caramelized by the sizzling hot iron to form simple and attractive criss-cross patterns and other designs.

Glazing irons, which resemble truncated pokers, are available from shops that supply professional catering equipment.

Alternatively, you could try holding a long meat skewer in a hot flame and then, while the skewer is still very hot, pressing it onto the sugar to create similar patterns.

Hot Clarified Butter

An attractive professional shine can be achieved by painting hot clarified butter over the lids and edges of hot savoury pies and tarts just prior to serving.

Jam Glazes

Open fruit tarts can be given an excellent gloss and flavour by warm jam glazes, which can also be brushed over the edges of pastry to give flavour as well as colour to finished tarts. Use yellow jams, such as peach, apricot or crabapple, for light-coloured fruits and redcurrant jelly for red and dark-coloured fruits.

Apricot Glaze

7oz/200g apricot, quince or crabapple jam
4oz/115g sugar
2fl oz/75ml water
1 tbsp lemon juice
Heat the jam, sugar, water and lemon juice until it is the consistency of syrup. Press the mixture through a sieve and use, while it is still warm and fluid, to paint over fruits.

Redcurrant Glaze

6oz/175g redcurrant jelly
1 tbsp water
Melt the jelly, stirring it gently to break up the lumps but do not whisk it or it will cloud. Do not cook for more than 1-2 minutes after melting, or the jelly will darken unpleasantly. If necessary, reheat gently to melt until fluid, then use to paint over the fruit.

DUSTING ICING SUGAR PATTERNS WITH STENCILS

A light dusting of icing sugar over the surface of a less than perfectly made or a simply decorated pie will enhance its appearance and cover a multitude of sins. Lay a stencil of a flower, shell or other pretty motif over a plain pie, sift icing sugar lightly over the surface and carefully lift off the stencil to reveal the sugary pattern (see Christmas Cranberry Pie, page 84).

LINING BAKING TINS AND BAKING BLIND

Careful, unhurried handling and chilling will produce a relaxed pastry that will shrink less in the oven and give better shaped pies and tarts. Lightly grease and flour the tins before lining them with the pastry.

Lining a Flan Tin

Roll out the pastry thinly until it is about 2in/5cm larger all round than the tin. Loosely roll the pastry around the rolling pin and unroll it over the tin. Hold the overlapping pastry in one hand while you ease the pastry into the contours of the tin, using your other hand to press it gently into shape. Use a small ball of floured pastry to press the pastry into the corners, especially if you are using a fluted tin.

Avoid stretching the pastry at all costs, because it will shrink back during baking. Fold the excess pastry evenly over the rim of the tin, then finish off the edges (see below). It is generally better to use a metal flan tin with a removable base rather than a china one, because heat is conducted more quickly through metal, so that the pastry not only cooks more thoroughly but is easier to turn out.

Finishing Edges

If you are using a plain ring trim the pastry just above the ring with a knife or scissors and knock up the edge. Use pastry pinchers to added a beaded edging or, if the flan is to have a lattice finish, leave it plain.

If you a using a fluted ring place the bent forefinger of one hand against the pastry inside the edge of the ring. Press the thickness of the pastry against your forefinger with the thumb of the other hand to flatten the top edge against the finger while you slowly rotate the tin. A small, inner lip of about $\frac{1}{4}$in/5mm will be formed level with the rim. Run your rolling pin firmly over the top to cut off neatly any scrap of pastry and leave a clean, level edge. Prick the base over with a fork to release any trapped air and leave to chill for 30 minutes.

Lining Individual Tartlet Tins

Place a tartlet tin upside down on the rolled-out pastry and cut around it, following the shape exactly but leaving a margin of about $\frac{1}{2}$in/12mm all round. Lift the pastry shape onto the tin and ease it inside, pressing the pastry down with a small ball of floured dough. Roll off any excess pastry with a rolling pin. Prick the base of the case and leave to chill for 20 minutes.

Lining Barquette Moulds

Set about 6 barquette moulds closely together; it is sometimes possible to buy them attached in a single sheet. Use your rolling pin to drape the thinly rolled-out pastry over the moulds. Ease the pastry into the moulds, shaping it neatly into the impressions with a small ball of floured dough. Run a rolling pin firmly over the tops of the moulds to cut off the excess pastry and then remove any pastry that is clinging to the edges of the moulds by running your thumb nail around the shapes. Prick the base of each mould and chill thoroughly before baking.

Lining Terrine and Game Pie Tins

See the individual recipes for Potato Pie (page 30) and Spoils of the Field Pie (page 66).

Pastry Dummies

Writing in *Pudding and Pastry à la Mode* in 1772 Mrs De Salis remarked: 'To keep tartlets and cheesecakes in good shape, a dummy should always be placed in each.' The dummies to which she was referring were formed from a paste made of equal proportions of flour, lard and water, which was divided into equal portions and moulded into round shapes. These shapes should, Mrs De Salis thought, be the size of the thickest half of an egg. They were then pinched in at the waist, and a small handle was made by squeezing the centre into a point about ¼in/5mm long. The dummies were then baked in the oven until firm and kept until required.

Before baking, one dummy would be placed in each tartlet and removed when the tartlet was cooked.

Nowadays baking blind is easier. Porcelain or metal baking beans are available from good kitchenware shops, or you can equally successfully use dried beans, dried rice or broken macaroni, which can be kept and used again.

Baking Blind

Line the tins with pastry (see above) and then, depending on the weight of the beans, place a layer or two of soft kitchen tissue over the pastry. Whenever possible I use the tissue that baker's bread is wrapped in because it is so soft and thin. Some people use kitchen foil or greaseproof paper, but I find that these tend to mark the pastry. Fill the pastry case with baking beans almost level to the top and bake according to the instructions given in the individual recipes.

ROLLING PINS AND OTHER GADGETS FOR DECORATIVE PASTRY

In the sixteenth century rolling pins decorated with figures from nursery rhymes or motifs in the shapes of flowers, animals or birds were often used to impress patterns onto gingerbread or small biscuits, which were afterwards frequently finely gilded with gold leaf.

By the nineteenth century rolling pins were usually plain, and they were generally made of sycamore, which did not colour or flavour food. Porcelain rolling pins were also made, and these could be filled with water to give extra weight and to keep the pastry cool while it was being rolled. A more utilitarian rolling pin was made in the early twentieth century of thick, clear glass. There were corks or stoppers at each end so that it could be filled with cold or iced water to keep the pastry cool while it was being rolled out.

It is perhaps hard for us to believe that these simple kitchen utensils were used as love tokens in the nineteenth century. It became fashionable for departing sailors to give their loved ones colourful glass rolling pins, many of which were filled with salt for weight. They were hung with ribbon or string near to the fire to keep the salt dry and to remind their users of their sweethearts. Another type of nineteenth-century rolling pin was ridged so that it could be used to crush oatmeal and coarse salt. These sometimes turn up in antique shops, and modern versions are stocked in some kitchenware shops. They can be used to make criss-cross patterns on pastry.

Another way of impressing patterns with a rolling gadget is to use a modern lattice cutter to make even cuts in the pastry, which can be gently eased open with the fingers of both hands. The trellis pattern thus formed can be laid over sweet of savoury fillings as a decorative crust, which opens out more during cooking to reveal the mouthwatering filling. This kind of crust is ideal for fruit and mincemeat tartlets, sausage rolls and beef Wellington.

Highly ornate rods of wood, which once graced the polished bannisters of fine Victorian staircases, can, when they have been suitably modified, make decorative rolling pins, which are particularly suitable for biscuit making.

MAKING DECORATIVE MOTIFS FOR SWEET PIES AND TARTS

Whenever possible, choose a motif that is appropriate to the ingredients in the filling – for example, an edging of pastry tomato leaves would complement the Tomato, Chilli and Pine Nut Tart (page 38), while oak and maple leaves would suit the Squirrel Treat Pie with Autumn Leaves (page 74). When you make the following, use pastries that keep their shape well during cooking.

In France exquisitely formed pastry roses entwined with diamond-patterned leaves are traditionally used to garnish savoury pâtés in pastry crusts, and pastry flowers always make a pretty addition to sweet pies and tarts.

Roses

You will find it helpful to study a real rose so that you can make the pastry version look as realistic as possible.

Take a piece of pastry about the size of a hazelnut and mould it into an elongated pyramid. Take a second piece, about twice as large as the first, and shape it into a rounded petal. Moisten the bottom half of the petal with a little egg wash and wind it around the pyramid. Gently bend back the edge of the petal and seal it at the base. Cut out 6-7 more pastry circles and press them into petal shapes. Moisten the second petal at the base and fold it around the first, lightly pinching and easing the pastry away from the centre. Add the remaining petals in the same way, shaping them and placing them around the bud so that they look as delicate and realistic as possible. Finally, squeeze the base of the rose lightly together to seal the shape, open up the flower a little more if you think it necessary and leave to chill thoroughly. Carefully egg wash the petals with a small brush and press onto the pastry lid before baking according to the recipe. To bake separately – for a game pie, for example – stand upright in crinkled kitchen foil.

Daisies

The daisy has been formed and baked in a small, Victorian, flower-shaped

biscuit tin. Bake in a preheated oven at 375°F/190°C/gas mark 5 for 8 minutes, remove from the mould and carefully paint over with egg wash. Return to the oven for a further minute to glaze.

To make a circular daisy follow the instructions for the circular coil given in meat and poultry decorations (see below), but press a small roll of pastry into the hollow of the coil to form the centre of the flower.

Leaves

One of the best ways of making realistic looking leaves is to press a well-shaped and heavily veined leaf from the garden firmly into rolled-out pastry, taking care not to pierce the dough. Use a sharp knife to cut around the leaf template, removing the excess dough from around the leaf before you pull it away. If necessary, strengthen the impressions of the veins with a knife or a wooden toothpick.

For this kind of fine work use a pastry that keeps its shape well during cooking – pâté sucrée is suitable for sweet pies, and pâté brisée can be used for both sweet and savoury dishes. Chill the shapes well before you attach them to pie lids for baking. If you are cooking the leaves separately – for use on decorative tartlets, for example – thinly glaze with egg wash and bake on a lightly greased baking tray at 375°F/190°C/ gas mark 5 for 5-6 minutes.

A simpler way is to use a leaf-shaped cuter to stamp out the leaves and then to mark the veins with a wooden toothpick or the back of a small knife. Leaf-shaped cutters are available in kitchenware shops, but look out for Victorian and Edwardian ones, which have more attractive shapes.

Diamond-shaped leaves, which are childishly simple to make, are traditionally used with roses on pâté pies. Cut rolled-out pastry into strips 1in/2.5cm wide and then cut across the strips at an angle at intervals of 1in/2.5cm to make diamonds. Use the back of a knife to mark the veins and pinch in one end to form a stalk before you fix them to the crust. Make them from pâté brisée, rich shortcrust or hot water crust.

Butterfly

Use thin card to make a template in the shape of a butterfly with a wing span of about 3in/7.5cm. Cut out the shapes from thinly rolled-out and chilled pâté sucrée and set them on a greased baking tray. Add 2 little strips to the head to represent antennae and use a sharp, pointed knife to mark the veins on the wings. Shape the body into a small elongated roll, tapered at one end. Add 4 tiny buttons of plain or chocolate pastry to the wings for decoration. (Make chocolate pastry by kneading a little chocolate powder into a small piece of pâté sucrée.) Alternatively, add a little red food colour to the pastry to tint the buttons. Bake unglazed in a preheated oven at 375°F/190°C/gas mark 5 for 8 minutes. Remove the biscuits from the oven, leave them to cool slightly and carefully paint over a fine layer of egg wash. Return to the oven for a further 2 minutes or until the biscuits look attractively glazed.

Serve as an accompaniment to summery puddings such as fruit compote or syllabub.

DECORATIONS FOR MEAT, GAME, POULTRY AND VEGETABLE DISHES

Creative and imaginative decorations can make an ordinary pie extraordinary. Because this intricate work requires very precise cutting, you should use a very sharp knife or a scalpel. The following decorations are suitable for use with most pastries unless otherwise indicated.

Rabbit

Pastry motifs shaped in the form of animals or birds are novel embellishments for pies and instantly inform the diner in a most attractive way of what lies beneath the crust. These motifs must be skilfully executed or they will look sadly unprofessional and badly done. Before you begin, look for visual references – well-illustrated children's books are extremely useful.

When you have found a suitable image, copy it onto tracing paper then transfer the drawing to thin card. Cut around the card to make a template. Roll out the pastry to approximately twice the thickness of the pie lid and, using the template as a guide, cut out the outline of the animal with a scalpel. Use your reference illustration to etch additional details with a pointed knife or add very thin strips to pastry to build up the features.

This kind of decoration works best with shortcrust or pâté brisée.

Tassels

Tassels make very pretty centre-pieces to meat or game pies.

To make a standard tassel cut a strip of pastry 1-1½in/2.5-4cm wide and 9in/23cm long and make a series of cuts about ⅛in/3mm apart. Roll up the strip and seal the uncut end with egg wash. Squeeze the end lightly with your fingers to splay out the pieces a little and set it onto the pie, easing out the strips if necessary with the end of a small paintbrush.

A spiral tassel can be made by cutting a strip of pastry 1-1½in/2.5-4cm wide and 9in/23cm long and make diagonal cuts about ¼in/5mm apart along one side. Roll up the strip tightly at the uncut end and seal it with a little egg wash. Gently squeeze the base and set it onto the pie with a little more egg wash. Lightly ease the

strips into position with the end of a small paintbrush if necessary.

Make a palm tassel by cutting a strip of pastry 1½in/4cm wide and 9in/23cm long. Make long, pointed, triangular cuts at regular intervals along one side of the strip, then roll it up tightly, sealing it with a little egg wash at the uncut side. Ease out the spiky pieces into an attractive palm-shaped tassel.

Moons and Crescents

Use a circular, fluted biscuit cutter 2in/5cm in diameter to cut out circles and crescents from the pastry, which should be rolled to twice the thickness of the pastry lid. Firmly impress a neat criss-cross pattern over the pastry shapes with a knife. These decorations are particularly suitable for puff pastry.

Peapods

Use pastry peapods to decorate the lids of vegetable pies or of the Peapod Pie (see page 40). Cut 2 long ovals, 4in/10cm long and 1in/2.5cm across at the widest point, from the rolled-out pastry, preferably shortcrust, wholemeal or pâté brisée. Make 9 tiny, pea-like balls of pastry, remembering that peas in a pod are not all the same size. Press the balls in a row over one of the lightly moistened ovals. Cut the remaining oval in half lengthways. Press one half over each side of the pastry base,

leaving the central line of peas partly exposed so that it resembles a split peapod. Pinch the ends of the shape into points and twist one point to form a stem. Make more peapods and some leaves and a trailing stem, cut and formed from the pastry, as required.

Mushrooms

Cut a simple outline of a mushroom from thin card and place your template on the rolled-out pastry. Cut around the template and decorate the surface of the pastry mushroom by making a neat criss-cross pattern with the blunt side of a knife, taking care not to pierce the pastry.

You could make several templates for different sizes and shapes of mushroom if you wished.

Roses and Diamond-shaped Leaves

These are traditionally used to decorate game pies; see Roses, Leaves and Butterflies on pages 19–21.

Spiral of Leaves

This pretty centre-piece can be easily made by pressing leaves, stamped out with a pastry cutter, around a central core of pastry.

Circular Coil Centre-piece

Cut an oblong of pliable but well-chilled, rolled-out pastry and make a series of evenly spaced cuts along the

centre, leaving a margin of ¼in/5mm of uncut pastry around all four edges. Moisten the 2 long edges with egg wash and fold the pastry loosely, pressing the dampened edges together. Form the folded strip into a circle, trimming it to fit if necessary, and press the flat, central edges together to make the coil. Chill the shape thoroughly before carefully transferring it on a palette knife to the centre of a pie. Alternatively, cook it separately to cover the central hole of a cooked game pie.

The circular coil can also be made into a daisy to decorate sweet pies. Simply add a small coil of pastry to the centre of the shape (see Circular Daisy page 21).

DECORATIONS FOR FISH AND SEAFOOD DISHES

Fish make wonderful motifs for decorating fish pies and seafood dishes, but you should also consider incorporating shells into your decorations. Shells have been a source of inspiration to artists for centuries, and have been used on glass, wood, stone and canvas. Shell-shaped pastries make the most attractive and elegant decorations for a variety of savoury and sweet dishes, and they can be easily adapted from ready-made moulds and real shells. These decorations are suitable for pastries that keep their shape well during cooking.

Fish

It is well worth making the effort to track down a well-formed fish mould, either new or antique, to help you visualize the shape you want to achieve. This is much easier than trying to copy a picture of a real fish, because the mould will be slightly abstract and stylized and you will find it easier to adapt to pastry. Draw a simple outline on card, making it an appropriate size for the pie lid, and cut it out. If you want to use a pastry fish as a single garnish for seafood served on a standard dinner plate, draw and cut out a template about 5in/12.5cm long. Carefully place your template on the pastry, which should be rolled out a little more thickly than the pie lid, and use a sharp knife or scalpel to cut out the shape.

Decorate the body of the fish following your sample pattern. Scales can be made with the end of a ¼in/5mm plain piping nozzle, which you can use to impress small semicircles into the pastry, or you could use the end of a potato peeler to make a pattern of Vs over the fish's body.

Use the blunt side of a knife to impress lines on the gills and fins. If you wish, you can make the gills from a separate piece of pastry, which can be pressed on over the pattern of scales. Finally, decorate the head, using a knife to impress the details. Alternatively, use very thin strips of pastry rather than cutting lines. Add an eye, made from two tiny circles, one smaller than the other.

A fish can also be shaped in a small tin mould, and the lines of the impression slightly strengthened with a modelling tool or knife.

Shells

Shell-shaped moulds made of clear plastic make excellent moulds for decorating fish pies.

Press small wedges of moist dough – pâté brisée for savoury dishes or pâté sucrée if you are decorating a sweet dish – into each of the moulds until the dough is level with the top of the mould. Leave to harden in the freezer, preferably overnight. To remove the shells, run the moulds briefly under tepid water and press your fingers firmly over the back of the moulds. Leave the shapes until they are almost defrosted, then press them over the top of the pastry lid. Lightly egg wash and cook at the temperature given in the recipe.

If you prefer to cut out the shapes, roll out the pastry a little more thickly than you would for the lid of the pie and then, using a circular, fluted biscuit cutter 2in/5cm in diameter, cut out a circle. Use a sharp knife to cut away a small slice from one side of the circle to leave a straight edge, and cut away 2 Vs from just below the straight edge to make the characteristic scallop shell shape. Press the back of a small, pointed

knife into the pastry to simulate the ribs of the shell. Press onto the pastry lid and bake as directed in the recipe.

Filled shells can be prepared in a similar way, but for these you will need 2 sheets of rolled-out pastry. Evenly space small mounds of savoury filling on the surface of one of the sheets of pastry, then use a pastry brush to paint a little egg wash around each mound. Lay the second sheet of pastry over the top. Carefully cut out the circles, forming them into shell shapes as before. This method can also be used successfully for filled pasta shapes.

Scallop Shell
Pastry can be formed and baked over real shells, either to make larger shells for use as containers for seafood or to make garnishes for cooked fish dishes.

Choose a scallop shell, with its pretty, rounded, open-fan shape, and grease it well on the outside with melted butter. Lay it on a baking sheet and press over it a piece of thinly rolled-out pastry, a little larger than the shell, making sure that the pastry is pressed firmly between the ribs of the shell. Use a sharp knife to cut round the edges, leaving $\frac{1}{2}$in/ 12mm of pastry all round. Leave to chill and rest in the fridge for at least 20 minutes. Trim off the excess pastry from around the edges and carefully paint a thin line of egg glaze down each rib of the pastry shell. For a

deeper colour, use saffron egg wash (see pages 15–16). Bake at 375°F/ 190°C/gas mark 5 for about 20 minutes and then carefully remove the pastry. Use shortcrust or pâté brisée. See page 42 for filo pastry shell containers or garnishes.

Starfish
A real dried starfish of the kind you can buy in some seaside gift shops is essential if you want to get the shape as realistic as possible. Do not use a star-shaped cutter – you will end up with something more suitable for hanging from your Christmas tree.

Roll out the pastry so that it is twice as thick as the pastry lid. Press the knobbly front of the starfish into the pastry until it leaves an impression, then use a sharp knife to cut around the outline, making the edge slightly undulating so that it looks as realistic as possible. Chill well before pressing over a pie lid, combining it with other nautical and marine decorations if you wish. Carefully paint over a thin coat of egg glaze and bake as directed in the recipe.

Mussel
Make a template of a mussel shell from thin card and use it to cut out a base shape from the rolled-out pastry. Cut out four more shapes, but make each one slightly smaller than the one before. Egg wash the shapes and press

them, one over the other, onto the base shape, with the smallest piece on top. Chill and follow the instructions in the recipe.

Horn Shell
You should make 2 at a time. Cut a strip of pastry $1\frac{1}{2} \times 13$in/4×33cm and lay a ruler between a point $\frac{1}{8}$in/3mm in from the left along one narrow end and a point $\frac{1}{8}$in/3mm from the right along the opposite narrow end. Cut along the ruler so that you have 2 long, wedge-shaped pieces of pastry.

Make the first shell by carefully wrapping the narrower end of the pastry strip around the tip of a greased tin horn mould, then continue to wind the pastry towards the wide end, overlapping each strip slightly and pressing the seams lightly together. Cut the end of the strip into a curve to simulate the appearance of a real horn-shaped shell. Make the second shell with the other piece of pastry, repeating the process as often as required. Smaller pastry horns can be made with shorter strips of pastry.

Paint a fine line of egg wash around the edges of the strips, lay the horns on their sides on a lightly greased baking tray and bake at 375°F/190°C/ gas mark 5 for 15 minutes.

Add hot or cold fish fillings to the horns. Smaller horns can be used with other pastry shell shapes to decorate fish pies and special seafood dishes; see Seafood in Seashell Sauce, page 42.

Rope and Plaits

To make a rope cut a portion of dough into 2 and make 2 thin sausage shapes, using your hands to roll out the dough to elongate it evenly. Remember that the twisting together will take up extra pastry, so roll out the pastry until it is longer than you think you will need. Twist the pieces together and seal at both ends before pressing into position over the egg-washed surface of the pie. Follow the chilling directions in the recipe.

Plaits are made from 3 strips, which should be ¾in/2cm wide. The strips should be at least 3in/7.5cm longer than the circumference of the pie; the extra length will be taken up in the plaiting. Lay the strips on a working surface and pinch them together at one end. Start plaiting at that end. Take the piece on the right and lay it over the piece in the centre. Take the piece on the left and lay it over the piece that is now in the centre. Continue in this way – right over centre, left over centre – until the plait is complete, then seal as before. Place on the egg-washed surface of the pastry lid and chill and bake as directed in the recipe.

MOULDING AND BAKING DECORATIVE PASTRY SHAPES

When you have the time and inclination there are a number of ways – simple and elaborate – of following the pleasurable art of moulding and baking to create small pastry decorations that can be used to enhance, in a very special way, the appearance of open-faced fruit tarts, fresh fruit puddings and poached fruits. You will have to search in bric-à-brac shops and antique markets for small, beautiful old moulds. Do not buy jelly moulds, but look out for the smaller moulds that were produced to make chocolate, marzipan and sorbet shapes. They are made of copper, tin or pewter, and they are often beautifully patterned with flowers, fruits, vegetables, shells and other exquisite shapes.

Look out, too, for wooden butter moulds, which are quite rare these days but can still be found. These were made in a range of mostly rustic designs, including swans, corn sheaves, thistles, cows and strawberries, which were used to identify the farm producing the butter. For example, swans on the wooden stamp indicated a dairy farm with water meadows, while a strawberry was used to identify a dairy farm that also grew fruit.

Victorian tartlet and biscuit tins were produced in a wealth of highly decorative designs, and these can be still be used. They sometimes turn up in bric-à-brac shops and in jumble sales, and you should keep an eye out for small, shallow, individual tins, which are usually tied together in piles of assorted shapes, still greasy and blackened from use in the days when baking was a daily event. These tins often have wonderfully intricate patterns – ornate crescents, hearts, flowers and shells – which are generally far better than their modern counterparts, and they are ideal for moulding sweet pastry decorations. If you come across these tins, inspect them carefully, because they may be made of tinned copper, which was produced to mould chocolate. These are collectors' items and can be quite valuable. If they find their way to antique shops it is possible that they will be sold with the tinned outer surface removed to reveal the highly polished copper, which makes them into attractive kitchen ornaments. If you think that your dull grey tin moulds have an inner lining of copper, make a deep scratch on the outside. If a warmer coloured metal shows through, it will be copper. Alternatively, use a magnet – copper is not attracted to magnets.

These highly decorated moulds are ideal for shaping pieces of pastry dough, but only those made of tin should be used for cooking.

Modern Moulds

Decorative biscuit tins and chocolate moulds are available in well-stocked kitchenware shops. Small chocolate moulds come in clear, plastic sheets, and there are generally six impressions.

Biscuit moulds are produced in some pretty designs, which are clearly copies of the Victorian models, but the choice is somewhat limited. You might also use decorative ice cube moulds, which are more widely available in the USA than in Britain but which are well worth finding. These soft, flexible moulds, usually in sheets of six impressions, are in the form of fish, shells or flowers.

MADELEINE MOULDS
These tin moulds are a constant inspiration. They are available in two sizes – small (1in/2.5cm) for petit fours and standard (2in/5cm) for the traditional French madeleines – and both are ideal for making elegant, shell-shaped pastries, which can be paired and filled with a variety of piped flavoured creams.

USING AND BAKING WITH MOULDS

Tin Moulds
Press dough into each tin until it is level with the top. Chill until firm then bake for 8 minutes. Turn out the shapes and lightly paint over with egg wash. Return to the oven for 1-2 minutes to glaze.

Rubber Moulds
Press a small piece of pâté sucrée carefully into each impression until the dough is level with the top of the mould.

Leave in the fridge for at least an hour, then carefully press your fingers over the back of the mould to ease out the shapes, which should be firm. Bake the shapes on a lightly greased tray at 375°F/190°C/gas mark 5 for 5 minutes until they are lightly golden around the

edges. Egg wash lightly and return to the oven for 1 minute to glaze. For an even better impression, place the filled moulds in the freezer and cook from frozen (having removed the moulds).

Clear Plastic Chocolate Moulds
Press small pieces of dough into each impression until the dough is level with the top of the mould. Place the filled sheet in the freezer, uncovered, until the dough is rock hard or, better still, leave overnight. Remove the moulded pastry by briefly running tepid water over the back of the moulds, then pressing your fingers firmly over the back of the plastic to snap the shapes free. Cook

from frozen as above, then carefully paint with egg glaze and return to the oven for a further minute or so until golden around the edges.

If you are using copper chocolate moulds, ease out the frozen dough by placing the tip of a pointed knife between the edge of the tin and the dough. Cook as above.

Old Wooden Butter Moulds
Shape some freshly made pastry into a pancake about ½in/12mm deep and a little larger than the mould and lightly press over the mould. Leave in the fridge to become slightly firm, then carefully peel the pastry away from the mould. This should leave a perfectly impressed motif over the surface of the pastry. Re-chill until firm, then cut away the excess pastry from around the patterned circle. This will make a superb decorative crust when it is set over an individual fruit pie. It is also ideal for shortbread or pâté sucrée biscuits to accompany poached fruit.

DECORATING THE EDGES OF PIES
The edges of covered pies can be finished in a number of different and attractive ways, ranging from a simple lined pattern made with the prongs of a fork to a frieze of finely moulded rose leaves or a more sumptuous sunburst pattern, in which the pastry is cut into points to simulate tiny sunrays (see page 10).

Whatever pattern you choose, it is important that the pie always has a double thickness of pastry around the edge. Lined pies will already have a double layer, but if only a top crust is to be used you will need to press a dampened strip of pastry around the rim of the pie dish before you add the pie lid.

For best results always use moist, supple and freshly made pastry that has been rested and chilled according to the recipe. Dry, over-stored and over-handled pastry will crack and crumble and look untidy.

For straight, even edges you must avoid shrinkage, which means that the pastry must be handled carefully and not stretched unnecessarily. Loosely roll the rolled-out pastry around your rolling pin and place it carefully over the pie, unrolling it into place. When you press the edges together, always ease the pastry inwards slightly, towards the centre of the pie, rather than pulling it back over the edges so that there is no 'give' in the pastry. It also helps if you trim the edges of the pie with scissors first, leaving a margin of about $\frac{1}{4}$in/5mm all round.

Rest the pie in the fridge before trimming the excess pastry close to the edge with a sharp knife, which should be held at a slight angle away from the dish. Do this before you decorate so that you can use the scraps to make the motifs.

Scalloped

This is one of the simplest of edges to make but also one of the most effective. Roll out the pastry, cover the pie dish, chill and trim the excess from around the edge. Gently press the forefinger of one hand onto the edge of the pastry, at the same time using the other hand to press the end of a lightly floured canalling knife or round-pointed knife at a slight angle into the pastry next to the finger. Work the pattern all the way around the edge.

Fluted and Forked

The simple forking method can be combined with a fluted pattern to make a very attractive edging. Roll out the pastry, cover the pie dish, chill and trim the edges. Flute the edge of the pastry by pressing it outwards with the forefinger of one hand and lightly pinching it inwards with the thumb and forefinger of the other hand. Repeat around the edge, keeping the round shapes evenly sized. Finish off by pressing into the each flute the back of a floured fork with the prongs pointed towards the centre of the pie.

Leaf and Flower

Roll out two-thirds of the pastry to cover the pie dish. Trim off the excess and press the scraps together with the remaining pastry to make the rose and leaf decoration (see pages 19–21). Brush the surface of the pie lid with egg glaze and carefully press the pastry leaves around the edge of the pie, remembering to leave a space for the rose. This type of decoration is especially suitable for sweet pies.

Twists and Braids

Make long, thin strips of pastry, twist or braid them (see page 26) and press them around the moistened edge of the pie lid. I find that this style of edging is suitable for fish pies, and pastry shells (see pages 24–25) can be used to disguise untidy joins. Use tassels (see page 22) or stars for other savoury fillings.

Gabled

This castellated pattern is very old, and it is used for game, pork and other savoury pies. Roll out the pastry, cover the pie, chill and trim. Use a sharp knife to make an even number of cuts about $\frac{1}{2}$in/12mm apart all the way round the edge. Fold alternate pieces of pastry inwards, while the remaining pieces are bent outwards.

Deco Sunburst

Follow the instructions for the gabled pattern, but when you have made the cuts all round the edge, use sharp scissors to snip off the corners of the pastry squares so that each one becomes a tiny triangle. Add a sunburst motif to the pie's surface if you wish. This kind of pattern can be used on most pies.

POTATO PIE

This handsome pie can be made in a round tin or in a terrine tin. The taste depends on just a few simple, fresh ingredients, which are encased in a buttery terrine of puff pastry and deliciously finished off with boiled cream.

Serves 6

EQUIPMENT
1 round tin with sloping sides 6in/15cm in diameter and $2\frac{3}{4}$in/7cm deep or 1 terrine tin 10 × 3in/25 × 7.5cm and $2\frac{3}{4}$in/7cm deep

INGREDIENTS
3oz/85g butter
5oz/140g onion, peeled and sliced
2lb/1kg new potatoes, peeled and sliced
2 tbsp parsley, freshly chopped
salt and freshly ground black pepper
1 quantity puff pastry made with 7oz/200g flour (see page 89)
egg glaze
5fl oz/150ml double cream

1. PREPARING THE VEGETABLES
Melt the butter and sauté the onions over a low to moderate heat for 3-4 minutes until they are soft and lightly coloured. Remove from the pan with a slotted spoon and leave on a china plate to cool. Add the potatoes, parsley and seasoning to the pan and cook for about 5 minutes until they are slightly softened. Leave to cool on a wire sieve.

2. USING THE ROUND TIN
Divide the pastry into 2 unequal pieces. Place the smaller piece in a plastic bag and return it to the fridge. Thinly roll out the larger piece to $12\frac{1}{4}$ × 10in/31 × 25cm. Use the base of a tin to cut out a circle from the exact centre of the pastry. Rinse the tin with cold water and shake out any excess. Place the circle of pastry over the bottom of the tin. Cut the remaining pastry into 2 strips to cover the inside edge of the tin, pressing the ends and base together and leaving the top edge slightly overlapping. Layer the cooled potato and onion in the lined tin, seasoning each layer, until the potatoes are level with the top. Roll out the pastry for a lid and trim away the excess around the edge. Cut a small hole in the centre and make decorations with the pastry scraps. Arrange these on the egg-glazed surface, then thinly paint the pastry surface with a second egg glaze before baking at 400°F/200°C/gas mark 6 for 1 hour. Loosely wrap a piece of kitchen foil over the pie shortly before the end of cooking if the pastry begins to brown. Insert a skewer through the hole to test if the potatoes are cooked. If they are, boil the cream and pour it slowly through a paper funnel into the pie. Leave to cool slightly before turning out.

3. USING THE TERRINE
Follow the method as above, but instead of dividing the pastry into 2, cut off 2oz/55g of dough and return it to the fridge in a plastic bag. Roll out the larger piece to $10\frac{1}{2}$ × 13in/ 27 × 33cm and cut it into 4 pieces, each $10\frac{1}{2}$ × $3\frac{1}{4}$in/27 × 8.25cm. Cover the base and long sides of the terrine with 3 of the pieces, leaving a small margin slightly overlapping the rim. Place the fourth piece, which will form the lid, in a plastic bag in the fridge. Roll out the 2oz/55g of dough and cut from it 2 pieces to cover the inside ends of the tin. Fill the pastry case with layers of potato and onion as above, but make a small circle at each end of the lid to add the cream and cut small slits along the surface of the pie instead of adding decorations.

QUAILS' EGG AND ASPARAGUS TARTLETS

The deliciously buttery sauce béarnaise goes beautifully with both the quails' eggs and the asparagus. These individual rich shortcrust pastry tartlets will make a perfect starter for an early summer dinner party.

Makes 4-6 individuals tartlets

EQUIPMENT
4 4½in/11cm plain, loose-bottomed tartlet tins, ¾in/2cm deep or 6 3¾in/9.5cm plain tartlet tins, ½in/12mm deep

INGREDIENTS
1 quantity shortcust made with 8oz/225g flour (see page 89)
12 quails' eggs
1lb/450g fresh asparagus
salt and pepper

FOR THE SAUCE BÉARNAISE
6oz/175g butter
1½ shallots, finely chopped
2 tbsp fresh tarragon, finely chopped
1 tbsp flat-leaf parsley, finely chopped
½ tsp white peppercorns, finely crushed
2 tbsp white wine vinegar
3 egg yolks
pinch of salt

1. MAKING THE PASTRY CASES
Thinly roll out the chilled pastry, line the tartlet tins and place them in the fridge for at least 20 minutes. Place a piece of soft paper towel inside each, fill with baking beans and bake blind for 15 minutes in a preheated oven at 375°F/190°C/gas mark 5. Remove the paper towel and baking beans and return to the oven for a further 10 minutes. Leave to cool slightly, then turn out onto a cake rack.

2. PREPARING THE ASPARAGUS
Steam the asparagus until it is tender, strain and cut off the spears, keeping the stalks to use in soup. Arrange the spears in the base of the tartlet cases and season. Set them aside while you make the sauce.

Because asparagus has such a short season, you can use mushrooms instead. Sauté them in butter with a dash of sherry, and add a pinch of mace, salt and freshly ground pepper just before the end of cooking.

3. MAKING THE SAUCE
Melt the butter very slowly in a small, thick-bottomed pan and leave to cool. Place the shallots, herbs, crushed peppercorns and vinegar into another small pan and boil vigorously until it has reduced to 1 dstsp of liquid. Remove from the heat, pour into a bowl or the top of a bain marie and add 1 tbsp of cold water. Mix the egg yolks and salt and add to the bowl with the vinegar mixture. Holding the bowl over simmering water, whisk for about 5 minutes until the mixture is creamy. Remove from the heat and add the cooled, melted butter, a little at a time, taking care not to add the milky sediment at the bottom. If the mixture becomes thick, add 1-2 tbsp of luke-warm water. When all the butter has been added, keep the sauce warm over a bain marie.

4. FILLING THE TARTLETS
Boil the quails' eggs for 2 minutes in boiling water. Refresh in cold water and shell them while they are still warm, cutting through both the shell and the thick skin beneath with a pointed knife. Place 3 eggs over the asparagus in each tart then spoon over the warm sauce. Add a little warm water to make the sauce smoother if necessary, but make sure that it retains its coating consistency.

Place the tartlets on a tray and place under a hot grill for 1 minute until the surface of the sauce begins to bubble and to look slightly scorched. Serve the tartlets piping hot.

MUSHROOM AND BRAZIL NUT PÂTÉ PIE

These beautiful, light nut-brown caps are grown in complete darkness before being shocked into pinning (turning into pinhead mushrooms) by careful changes of temperature.

Makes 1 9in/23cm pie

EQUIPMENT
1 9in/23cm tin pie plate

INGREDIENTS
1 quantity light wholemeal pastry made with 4oz/115g wholemeal and 4oz/115g plain flour, chilled (see page 91)
2oz/55g butter
2 small onions, finely chopped
3 garlic cloves, crushed
1 green pepper, deseeded and chopped
3oz/85g Brazil nuts, finely chopped
2 tbsp chopped parsley
1 tbsp mixed herbs
1¼lb/550g mushrooms, cubed
pinch of powdered mace
1oz/25g wholemeal breadcrumbs
3oz/85g gruyère cheese, grated
5 tbsp double cream
squeeze of lemon juice
1 tsp salt
freshly ground black pepper

1. LINING THE TIN
Divide the wholemeal pastry into 2 slightly uneven pieces, using the smaller piece to line the greased plate. Wrap the unused pastry in a plastic bag and replace it and the lined plate to the fridge to rest.

2. PREPARING THE FILLING
Melt the butter in a frying pan and sauté the onions and garlic over a low heat until soft and lightly coloured. Add the green pepper and Brazil nuts and stir-fry over a low to moderate heat for a further 3 minutes. Add the herbs, mushrooms, spice, breadcrumbs and cheese and cook for a further 2 minutes. Finally stir in the cream and lemon juice and season to taste. Leave to cool before spreading evenly over the pastry-lined plate.

3. COVERING THE PIE
Roll out the remaining pastry and cover the pie dish. Trim and decorate the edge, then decorate the top with the moistened scraps, re-rolled and pressed over the lightly egg-washed lid. Set on a preheated tray to help cook the base of the pie evenly and bake at 375°F/190°C/gas mark 5 for 30-35 minutes. When the pie has cooled, leave it in the fridge, preferably overnight, until the filling has a firm, pâté-like texture. Serve as a cold *pâté en croute* with a crisp green salad.

VEGETABLE GOULASH AND BLACK-EYED BEAN PIE

The art lies in not over-cooking the vegetables so that they contrast deliciously with the tomato coulis, which is lightly flavoured with garlic and curry.

Serves 6

EQUIPMENT
1 10½-11in/27-28cm round pie tin or heatproof dish, 1½in/4cm deep

INGREDIENTS
1 quantity light wholemeal pastry made with 4oz/115g wholemeal and 4oz/115g plain flour (see page 91)

FOR THE VEGETABLE AND BEAN FILLING
2 large parsnips, peeled, halved and cut into ½in/12mm slices
2 large carrots, peeled, halved and cut in ½in/12mm slices
½ small swede, peeled and cut into ½in/12mm thick wedges
2 leeks, cleaned and sliced
3 courgettes, cut into ½in/12mm slices
4 medium potatoes, peeled and each cut into 8 pieces
1oz/25g butter
1 large red pepper, deseeded and cut into 1in/2.5cm pieces
6 large mushrooms, sliced
4oz/115g black-eyed beans, soaked overnight and cooked until tender

FOR THE TOMATO COULIS
3 medium onions, chopped
2 garlic cloves, crushed
2 tbsp extra virgin olive oil
1½ tbsp medium curry powder
2 14oz/400g cans chopped tomatoes
1 tbsp tomato ketchup
1 tbsp tomato purée
1 bay leaf
4 sprigs parsley, chopped
1 tsp salt

1. MAKING THE TOMATO COULIS
Sauté the onions and garlic gently in the oil until golden. Add the curry powder and leave to cook for a further 1 minute. Remove from the heat, cover and leave on one side. Place the tomatoes in a saucepan with the remaining ingredients for the coulis and leave to simmer until reduced by half, which should take about 20 minutes. Stir in the onion mixture and leave to simmer for a further minute. Remove from the heat.

2. PREPARING THE VEGETABLES
Bring a pan of salted water to the boil and cook the prepared vegetables – in separate batches – the parsnips, carrots and swedes for 4 minutes, the leeks and courgettes for 3 minutes and the potatoes for 6-7 minutes. Remove each set of vegetables from the boiling water with a slotted spoon and leave to one side before adding the next.

Melt the butter in a small frying pan and sauté the red pepper until tender. Add the mushrooms and stir-fry for a further minute. Stir all the vegetables with the cooked beans into the tomato coulis and turn gently in the sauce until well covered. Transfer to the pie tin or heatproof dish.

3. COVERING THE PIE
Thinly roll out the pastry and cover the pie. Make decorations with the trimmings and glaze with egg wash. Cook in a preheated oven at 375°F/190°C/gas mark 5 for 30-35 minutes or until the pastry looks nicely cooked and golden. The slightly coarse texture of the wholemeal pastry marries particularly well with the tender vegetables.

TOMATO, CHILLI AND PINE NUT TART

You could use red tomatoes instead of green ones, or use a combination of both ripe and unripened tomatoes.

Makes 1 10in/25cm tart; serves 4

EQUIPMENT
1 10in/25cm tart tin, with a lip approximately 1in/2.5cm wide

INGREDIENTS
1 quantity pâté brisée made with 8oz/225g flour (see page 93)
1 tbsp olive oil
3 shallots, finely chopped
1 fat garlic clove, crushed
2 tsp sweet chilli sauce
1 tbsp pine nuts
1lb/450g green tomatoes
4-5 basil leaves, torn into pieces
1oz/25g butter, cut into small pieces
½ tsp salt
freshly ground pepper

1. LINING THE TIN
Use about two-thirds of the chilled pastry to line the tart tin. Place the remaining pastry and any scraps, pressed together in a moist ball inside a plastic bag, in the fridge until required.

2. PREPARING THE VEGETABLES
Melt the oil in a frying pan and gently sauté the shallots with the garlic until golden. Stir in the chilli sauce, then add the pine nuts and leave to cook for a further minute. Remove from the heat and set to one side.

Slice the tomatoes thinly and arrange them over the base of the pastry-lined tin. Sprinkle over the torn basil leaves, then spread some of the pine nut and onion mixture over the top. Add another layer of sliced tomatoes and then the rest of the pine nut and onion mixture. Dot over the butter. Add salt and pepper to taste.

3. DECORATING THE TART
Roll out the remaining pastry and make pastry leaf decorations to go around the edge of the tart. Bake in a preheated oven at 375°F/190°C/gas mark 5 for 25-30 minutes.

This is delicious, served hot or cold, with waxy new potatoes or potatoes *à la dauphinoise* and crisply cooked French beans.

PEAPOD PIE

In fact, there are no peapods in this pie, which is named after the pastry decorations atop the lid. Freshly cooked garden peas are a great delicacy, especially as an accompaniment to tender lamb and waxy new potatoes cooked in mint.

Serves 4

EQUIPMENT
1 small or medium heatproof pie dish; the peas should come almost to the top of the dish

INGREDIENTS
3oz/85g butter
2 shallots or ½ large onion, finely chopped
1 garlic clove, crushed
6-7 young sorrel leaves
2lb/1kg fresh peas (to make 1lb/500g podded peas)
a sprig of freshly picked mint leaves, about 4in/10cm long
¼ pint/150ml chicken or vegetable stock
3 tbsp thick cream
4 small, garden-fresh lettuce leaves
salt
freshly ground black pepper
½ quantity standard wholemeal pastry or rich shortcrust made with 4oz/115g flour (see page 91)

1. PREPARING THE VEGETABLES
Add 1oz/25g of the butter to a medium sized frying pan and sauté the shallots (or onion) and garlic over a low heat until soft and lightly coloured. Tear the sorrel leaves into smallish pieces and stir into the shallot mixture, cooking over the same heat for a further minute.

Melt the remaining butter in the pan, then stir in the peas and mint and cook over a moderate heat, turning continually in the hot buttery juices, for about 1 minute. Add the stock, then the cream. Leave to bubble gently in the juices for 1-2 minutes more, then remove from the heat.

Place the lettuce leaves over the base and around the sides of the pie dish and pour in the contents of the pan. Season to taste and leave on one side to cool.

2. ASSEMBLING THE PIE
Only half the usual quantity of pastry is required because the pie is unlined. Roll out the pastry so that there is sufficient to make a thin strip to edge the pie dish, the pie lid and the peapod decorations (see page 23). Assemble the pie. If there are sufficient peas, they will support the weight of the pastry lid. Alternatively, use a pie funnel. Trim and decorate the edges. Place the pie in the fridge for 10 minutes until the pastry is firm, then give the whole surface another thin coat of egg glaze. Bake in a preheated oven at 400°F/200°C/gas mark 6 for 25 minutes until the pastry has a beautifully golden and shiny appearance.

Serve as an accompaniment to meat, poultry or fish. When they are the main ingredient of a pie or soup peas can be a little bland, but lemony-tasting sorrel leaves perfectly counteract their slight sweetness.

SEAFOOD IN SEASHELL SAUCE

These tiny, shell-shaped pastries, which are made from filo pastry, make wonderfully attractive garnishes to a host of special seafood dishes. Try making them in advance and storing them on a tray in the freezer for future use.

Serves 4

FOR THE FISH STOCK
2lb/1kg fish bones and trimmings
1 stick celery, chopped
1 medium onion, sliced
5fl oz/150ml dry white wine
6 peppercorns
bouquet garni

FOR THE PASTRY SHELLS
4 sheets of frozen filo pastry, 9 × 10in/
23 × 25cm (see page 92)
4 small, cleaned scallop shells
1oz/25g melted butter
egg glaze
4 small tin horn moulds

FOR THE FISH
1 medium sized crab
12oz/350g fresh prawns in shells
2oz/55g shelled cockles
4 scallops
4oz/115g cooked mussels

FOR THE SAUCE
2 tbsp shallot or 3 tbsp onion, chopped
1½oz/45g butter
4fl oz/100ml fish stock
4fl oz/100ml medium dry white wine
½ pint/300ml double cream

1. MAKING THE FISH STOCK
Add the ingredients to 2 pints/1 litre of water and bring to the boil. Simmer for 30 minutes, leave to cool and strain.

2. MAKING SCALLOP SHELLS
Cut 2 of the filo sheets into squares large enough to cover the scallop shells and cover the pastry with a damp cloth until you need to use it. Lightly butter the outside of the shells and cover each with a piece of pastry. Brush with melted butter, taking care to brush well down between each rib to help mould the pastry into the shell forms. Lay a second sheet of filo over the first and paint with egg glaze, pressing the brush well down as before. Trim away any excess pastry. Bake for 4 minutes in a preheated oven at 425°F/220°C/gas mark 7, then leave to cool on the shell moulds before peeling away.

3. MAKING HORN SHELLS
Follow the instructions on page 25 but use smaller strips of pastry, winding each piece halfway up the mould. Glaze and bake as above.

4. PREPARING THE FISH
You will need about 2oz/55g white crab meat altogether; keep it in whole pieces as far as possible. Peel the prawns. (Use the prawn shells and emptied crab shell in the stock.) Clean the cockles and remove the scallops from the shells, separating the bodies from the corals. Slice each into 4 pieces and set on one side with the corals and the prepared cockles and mussels.

5. MAKING THE SAUCE
Sauté the shallots or onion in the butter until soft but not coloured. Add the stock and wine and boil until reduced by half. Pour in the cream and reduce again until the liquid is the consistency of a light sauce. Reduce the heat to a low simmer and spoon the seafood into the sauce to warm through for 4 minutes. Stir lightly once or twice. Have ready 4 warmed plates and serve the seafood together with the pastry shells, which should be slightly warmed in the oven. If the sauce needs thickening, remove the shellfish and leave the liquid to reduce for a minute or less to the correct consistency. Garnish with fresh dill.

SALMON EN CROUTE

Although home-made puff pastry is always preferable, I suggest you buy ready-made frozen pastry for this recipe because the texture is firmer and easier to work when you cut out the shapes for the fish's scales, fins and so on.

Serves 8

INGREDIENTS
4-4 ½lb/2kg fresh salmon
1¼lb/550g ready-made puff pastry

FOR THE FILLING
3 sprigs of tarragon, parsley and dill
2oz/55g butter, softened
1 piece of fresh root ginger, 1in/2.5cm square, very finely chopped
1 tsp lemon juice
salt and black pepper
double quantity of Seashell Sauce (see page 42)

1. MAKING THE PASTRY CASE

Fillet the fish into 2 pieces. Remove the skin and reserve with the bones for the stock. Roll out about 5½oz/155g of the pastry into a slim oblong. Lay the fish fillets, one on the top of the other, in the centre of the pastry and cut around them, leaving a margin of about ¾in/2cm because the pastry shrinks during cooking. The pastry shape should look like the fish in its natural state, with a head and tail. Remove the fillets and place them to one side. Prick the pastry with a fork and place it on a large, dampened baking sheet. Bake for 20 minutes in a preheated oven at 425°F/220°C/gas mark 7. Remove from the oven and leave to cool on the baking sheet.

2. PREPARING THE BUTTER FILLING

Chop the herbs and mix them into the butter with the ginger and lemon juice. Season the fish and spread the flavoured butter between the fillets and over the top. Place the fish on the cooked pastry shape. Cut off another 5½oz/155g of pastry and roll it out thinly to cover both the fish and the base, leaving an overlap of ¾in/2cm. Tuck this margin under the base. Do not press the tail piece underneath; this can be pressed over the fish and trimmed to shape.

3. DECORATING THE FISH

Roll out all the remaining pastry and cut out the fins, gill and about 150 small circles for the scales. I use the end of a plain ¾in/2cm piping nozzle. You will also need some strips about ¼in/5mm wide for the tail and fins; use the moist pastry scraps, pressed together and re-rolled if necessary. Brush the surface of the pastry with egg wash. Decorate the tail with some of the trimmed strips. Add some of the circles to the body by pressing them, slightly overlapping each other, in a line running across the fish at the tail end. Follow this with a second line, which should slightly overlap the first line. There will be about 8 circles in a line. Continue to place the scales, brushing each with a little more egg wash until you reach the head, where you will need several semicircles to meet the decorative strips that go around the head and eye. Attach the fins and gill, and press over some more of the thin, trimmed strips to give a rib-like effect. Egg wash and chill for 20 minutes. Bake for 25 minutes at 425°F/220°C/gas mark 7; reduce the temperature to 375°F/190°C/gas mark 5 and bake for a further 15 minutes.

4. MAKING THE SAUCE

Follow the recipe for Seashell Sauce but double the quantities to make sufficient for 8 people.

CRAB WITH MARINADED SWEET PEPPERS IN FILO CASES

I particularly like these delicate filo cases. They make a light, piquant starter, each portion garnished with fresh dill and a single crab claw, or excellent canapés.

Makes 8 tartlets; serves 4 as a starter

EQUIPMENT
fluted tartlet tins, approximately 3½in/9cm across the top, 2½in/6cm across the bottom and ½in/12mm deep

INGREDIENTS
2 large red peppers
8oz/225g fresh white crab meat, or brown and white meat mixed

FOR THE MARINADE
2 garlic cloves, peeled and crushed
4 tbsp extra virgin olive oil
2 tbsp lemon juice
1 tsp sugar or clear honey
salt
freshly ground pepper

FOR THE FILO CASES
3 sheets ready-made, frozen filo pastry; you may need more depending on the size of the sheets or if you wish to make the small filo decorations to garnish the tartlets (see page 92)
1-2oz/25-55g butter

1. PREPARING THE PEPPERS
Heat the oven to 475°F/240°C/gas mark 9. Halve the peppers and discard the seeds. Lightly paint the skins with olive oil and lay, cut side down, on a baking tray. Bake for about 25 minutes, until charred and blistered. Wrap in a plastic bag until cool, when the skin should peel away quite easily. Cut the peppers into matchstick size strips and place them in a small bowl. Whisk together the ingredients for the marinade and stir into the peppers. Leave covered in the fridge for 1-2 hours, stirring occasionally.

2. MAKING THE FILO CASES
Paint melted butter over 1 sheet of pastry. Lay a second sheet on top, paint with butter and lay a third sheet on top. Use a round 3½in/9cm biscuit cutter to stamp out pastry circles from the 3-layered filo to line eight tartlet tins. Prick the bottom of the tartlets and bake for 6-8 minutes in a preheated oven at 375°F/190°C/gas mark 5. Leave to cool, then ease the tartlets from the moulds.

The tartlet cases can be made in advance and kept for a short period in an airtight container or, for longer, in the freezer. They take only 5 minutes to defrost at room temperature, but you can warm them in a low oven to re-crisp them if you think it necessary.

To make a filo decoration, cut 3 strips of filo pastry, about ½ × 5in/ 12mm × 12.5cm, and roll them loosely together into a coil. Ease out the 3 ends and use scissors to trim the ends to uneven lengths. Make as many decorations as you need, then leave them to dry a little before baking, flat side up, on a baking tray for 3-4 minutes until they are golden brown. Egg glaze and return to the oven for a further minute.

3. MAKING THE FILLING
Lightly break up the crab meat and add a small pile to the base of each cooked pastry case. Arrange the marinaded sweet peppers over the top and garnish with the filo decorations or small sprigs of fresh dill before serving.

Fidelity Intl Inv Mngt (Luxembourg) SA
Equitilink International Mngt Ltd
Fidelity Investment (CI) Ltd
Fleming Group
Foreign & Colonial Mngnt (Jersey) Ltd
Midland Internatl Circuit Fund SICAV (u)
The First Korea Smaller Companies Fund
Five Arrows Intl Bond Fund (u)
Fleming Group
Gartmore Luxembourg S.A.
Nomura Global Fund (u)
H.C.M. HYPO Capital Mgt Luxembourg SA
John Govett Management (Jersey)
INVESCO MIM International
International Bond Trust
INVESCO MIM International Limited
Latin American Management Co Ltd
Lloyds Bank Luxembourg (u)

SWEET SALMON PYE

This unusual recipe reminds me of those medieval pies in which the fish was often sweetened with currants and spices. Here cubes of fresh salmon are emulsified in a rich herby cream, which is subtly flavoured with ginger, currants and garlic.

Serves 4

EQUIPMENT
1 long, shallow oblong tin, 14 × 4 ½in/36 × 11cm or 1 10in/25cm round tin pie plate

INGREDIENTS
3 shallots, peeled and very finely chopped
2 fat garlic cloves, crushed
2oz/55g butter
1 quantity rich shortcrust made with 8oz/225g flour (see page 89)
1lb/450g fresh salmon, skinned and boned and cut into ½in/12mm cubes
1½oz/45g sultanas
2oz/55g crystallized stem ginger
sprig of fresh dill, chopped
sprig of parsley, chopped
salt
freshly ground black pepper
2-3 tbsp thick cream
egg glaze or saffron egg glaze

1. LINING THE TIN
Gently sweat the shallots and garlic in half the butter until soft and golden, then transfer them to a china plate to cool.

Divide the chilled pastry into 3 pieces. Thinly roll out 2 of the pieces. Line the tin with the first, reserve the second for the lid and return the third, in a plastic bag, to the fridge.

2. PREPARING THE FILLING
Layer the salmon in the uncooked pastry case with the sultanas, chopped ginger, herbs, seasoning and cooled shallot mixture. Pour over the cream and dot with the remaining butter.

3. DECORATING THE PIE
Dampen the edges of the pastry with egg wash and cover with a pastry lid. Gather and lightly press together the trimmings and cut from them and the remaining chilled pastry suitable fish decorations (see pages 24–5). Dampen the pastry lid with egg wash and press over the decorations. Paint over another thin coat of egg glaze or saffron egg glaze (see pages 14–16), which will give a deeper yellow, then bake in a preheated oven for 375°F/190°C/gas mark 5 for 25 minutes until the pastry is golden.

Serve with pretty salad leaves dressed in vinaigrette and waxy new potatoes garnished with chopped chives. This recipe also works well if you prefer to make four individual pies rather than one large one.

STARGAZEY PIE

*I have always been fascinated by this unusual recipe, which comes from Cornwall.
It was traditionally made with pilchards, and the fishes' inedible heads were left on
so that the oils in them could drain back into the fish while the pie cooked.*

Serves 6

EQUIPMENT
1 10½-11in/27-28cm tin or china plate

INGREDIENTS
*saffron egg glaze (see pages 14–16)
1 quantity shortcrust made with
12oz/350g flour (see page 89)*

FOR THE FILLING
*8 fresh sardines or herrings, 6in/15cm
long
2 small eggs
scant ¼ pint/150ml clotted cream
small handful green herbs, including
parsley and dill, chopped
8 rashers streaky bacon
salt
freshly ground black pepper
1 small onion, finely chopped*

1. PREPARING THE FISH
Gut the fish with a very sharp knife and remove the bones. Cut off the fins and tails with scissors and rinse thoroughly under cold, running water. Leave to drain on kitchen paper.

2. PREPARING THE GLAZE
Pour the milk into a small saucepan and bring to the boil. Remove from the heat, sprinkle over the saffron strands and leave to infuse for at least an hour. Mix in the egg yolk and salt.

3. PREPARING THE FILLING
Beat the eggs, cream and herbs together and set to one side. Add a good grinding of pepper and salt to the insides of the fish and wrap a rasher of bacon around each one.

Divide the chilled pastry into 2 uneven pieces. Thinly roll out the smaller piece to line the greased plate, returning the other piece with the gathered scraps in a plastic bag to the fridge. Arrange the bacon-wrapped fish in a radiating circle on the pastry-lined plate, with the tail ends touching in the centre. Sprinkle over the chopped onion, then pour over the herb custard, adding seasoning.

Dampen the edges of the pastry with egg wash. Roll out the second piece of pastry and cut a circle the same size as the plate. Carefully lay the pastry over the fish, pressing it down between the fish heads to seal. Use a sharp knife to cut away small semicircles of pastry to expose the fish heads.

4. DECORATING THE PIE
Dampen the pie lid with saffron egg glaze and press a rope decoration (see page 26) around the edge. Cut out the remaining pastry decoration from rolled-out scraps. You could make seashells or a starfish. Press the decorations on the pie lid and paint over with a second coat of glaze. Bake in a preheated oven at 400°F/200°C/gas mark 6 for 15 minutes then reduce the temperature to 350°F/180°C/gas mark 4 for a further 25-30 minutes until the pie looks crisp and golden. Serve immediately. A bowl of steaming-hot buttered spinach and creamed potatoes would be delicious accompaniments.

SPICY LAMB IN HERB PASTRY PURSES

This is an updated version of a traditional English recipe for mutton pie, which dates from the Middle Ages. It was one of the earliest versions of the modern sweet mincemeat pie. The meat was eventually omitted from the spicy fruit filling.

Makes 6 individual purses

EQUIPMENT
1¾in/4cm plain or fluted biscuit cutter

INGREDIENTS
1 quantity herb pastry made with 8oz/225g flour (see page 92)
egg wash

FOR THE FILLING
1 large onion, finely chopped
1oz/25g butter
12oz/350g shoulder of lamb, trimmed of some fat to make 9oz/250g in all
2 eating apples, peeled and grated
1 tsp orange zest
1 tbsp currants
½ tsp nutmeg, finely grated
salt
pepper

1. PREPARING THE FILLING
Lightly sauté the onions in butter until golden, then leave to cool. Mince the meat coarsely, place it in a mixing bowl and combine with the remaining ingredients. Season well and divide into 6 equal portions.

2. MAKING THE PASTRY PURSES
Cut the pastry into 6 equal pieces. Roll out one piece, keeping the remaining pastry in a plastic bag in the fridge, and cut out a circle 5½in/14cm in diameter, using a saucer as a template.
Press the trimmings into a small, moist ball and roll out. Use the biscuit cutter to cut a circle and decorate the pastry with the back of a knife.
   Form a portion of spiced lamb mix into a small ball and place it in the centre of the larger pastry circle. Egg wash the edge of the circle and pull it upwards, over the lamb, pressing the creased pastry together at the top to form a purse. Paint egg wash over the pastry and the smaller circle and press the smaller circle firmly over the small opening at the top of the purse to cover it.

Make the other 5 purses in the same way. Transfer the completed purses to a greased baking tray and bake in a preheated oven at 375°F/190°C/gas mark 5 for 30 minutes. Allow 2 purses per person for a light lunch or supper, when hot new potatoes and a crisp salad will be the perfect accompaniment. These are so delicious that it is worth doubling (or even trebling) the quantities so that you can store some in the freezer.

CHICKEN AND BUTTERBEAN HUFF

Choose 'Bonito' sweet potato for this dish. It has a pink skin and yellow flesh and is more elongated and twisted than usual potatoes. Their fragrant sweetness is an interesting complement to poultry and game.

Serves 4

EQUIPMENT
1 2 pint/1.1 litre round pie dish or pudding basin

INGREDIENTS
¾ pint/450ml chicken stock
pinch saffron strands
1 medium onion, sliced
4 corn-fed chicken breasts, skinned
small handful of thyme and parsley sprigs, chopped
several chives, roughly chopped
6oz/175g carrots, julienned
4oz/115g leeks, sliced
2oz/55g butterbeans, cooked
pinch cinnamon, powdered
salt and pepper to taste
1 yellow-fleshed sweet potato
1 large potato, peeled and cubed
1oz/25g butter
½ quantity flaky pastry (see page 90)
egg glaze

1. PREPARING THE CHICKEN

Add the stock, saffron strands and onion to a pan and bring to the boil. Leave to simmer briskly for 15 minutes.

Layer the chicken with the herbs, vegetables, butterbeans, cinnamon and seasoning in the dish and pour over the hot saffron and onion stock. Cover with a lid or kitchen foil and cook in a preheated oven at 350°F/180°C/gas mark 4 for 40 minutes, stirring halfway through. Remove from the oven and leave to cool.

2. PREPARING THE POTATOES

While the chicken is cooking, peel the sweet potato and cut it into 1in/2.5cm discs. Cook in boiling water for 15 minutes. Drain and mash thoroughly. Cook the ordinary potato until soft, then mash together with the sweet potato, the butter, seasoning and cinnamon.

Spread the mashed potato into a layer over the casseroled chicken. Cover with a lid of rolled-out pastry, cut into a circle with a ½in/12mm margin overlapping all round. Press the pastry edge down over the outside of the baking dish, and cut an air vent in the lid. Wash the surface of the pastry with egg glaze and bake in a preheated oven at 400°F/200°C/gas mark 6 for 30 minutes until the surface looks golden and glossy. Serve with mange-tout peas or French beans, cooked until just tender.

NOTE THREE LARGE S...
INVALUABLE FOR...

STEAK AND OYSTER PIE

*Oysters used to be regarded as poor man's food and were used in vast quantities
in everyday dishes. They were probably used in this pie to eke out the meat.
Happily for us, the unusual combination of meat and shellfish is delicious.*

Serves 4

EQUIPMENT
*1 oblong pie dish 11 × 7in/28 × 17.5cm
and 2in/5cm deep*

INGREDIENTS
*8 oysters
1 medium onion, peeled and chopped
2oz/55g butter
6oz/175g large mushrooms, sliced
1½lb/750g best lean steak, cut into small
cubes
4oz/115g kidney, trimmed and cut into
small cubes
1 rounded tbsp flour
small handful of parsley, chopped
1 very generous pinch ground black
pepper
salt to taste
½ pint/300ml beef stock
½ quantity puff pastry (see page 89)
rich egg glaze*

1. PREPARING THE OYSTERS
Open the oysters carefully with an
oyster knife, protecting your other
hand with a heavy-duty glove or
kitchen cloth. Place the oyster meat
and the strained liquor from the shells
in a small bowl and leave to one side.

The best way to keep oysters is to
wrap them in wet newspaper, flat side
upmost, and keep them in the fridge,
where they should keep for 2-3 days.
Any that have opened of their own
accord must not be used.

2. PREPARING THE FILLING
Gently sauté the onion in the butter in
a frying pan until golden, then stir-fry
the mushrooms until lightly coloured.
Use a slotted spoon to remove the
onion and mushrooms, allowing the
hot fat to drain back into the pan.
Leave to one side while you add the
steak and kidney to the pan. Toss the
meat lightly in the hot fat.

Add the flour and stir-fry for a few
minutes until the flour has
amalgamated with the meat juices.
Stir in the onion and mushrooms and
add the parsley, seasoning, stock,
oysters and liquor. Leave to bubble
gently for 2-3 minutes more, then

transfer the ingredients from the pan
to a medium sized saucepan and
leave, covered with a lid, to cook on a
low simmer for 1¼ hours. Stir
occasionally.

3. COVERING THE PIE
Use a slotted spoon to transfer the
contents of the pan to a pie dish,
leaving the juices in the pan to bubble
and thicken slightly until there is
enough almost to cover the meat in
the pie dish.

Wait until the meat is cool, insert a
pie funnel in the centre of the dish and
cover with a pastry lid. Chill briefly in
the fridge for about 15 minutes to firm
the pastry, coat with egg glaze and
bake in a preheated oven at 400°F/
200°C/gas mark 6 for 30-35 minutes
until the pastry is a rich golden
colour.

SAVOURY PIE

This failsafe recipe, which was given to me by my mother, has become a special teatime treat over the years. It combines mature cheddar cheese in the most delicious way with onion, salty bacon and tomatoes.

Serves 9

EQUIPMENT
*1 shallow baking tin 12 × 12in/
30 × 30cm or a Swiss roll tin or 2
shallow tins 4½ × 14in/11 × 36cm*

INGREDIENTS
*1 quantity rich shortcrust made with
8oz/225g flour (see page 89)
egg glaze*

FOR THE FILLING
*1 medium onion
12oz/350g green (unsmoked) back bacon
5oz/140g mature cheddar cheese
4 medium, slightly overripe tomatoes*

1. PREPARING THE FILLING
Mince together all the ingredients for the filling, preferably using an old, hand-operated mincer of the kind found in grandmother's kitchen cupboard. I find that this gives the right texture. If you use a liquidizer add small amounts to the goblet and blend into a fairly coarse mixture.

2. PREPARING THE PASTRY
Cut the chilled pastry into 2 pieces. Thinly roll out one piece and line the greased tin, leaving a small overlapping margin.
  Spread the filling evenly over the base of the pastry-lined tin. It will be a fairly thin layer, but it has a very strong flavour and you will not need too much of it. Thinly roll out the remaining piece of dough so that it is slightly larger than the tin and cut it with a lattice cutter or leave it plain. Dampen the edges with egg wash and press them together. Use a sharp knife to trim the edges neatly and lightly egg wash the surface. Decorate the lid with small pastry leaves made from the scraps. Leave to chill in the fridge to firm up the pastry, then apply another thin coat of egg wash over the surface. Bake in a preheated oven at 375°F/190°C/gas mark 5 for 30-35 minutes until the pastry looks golden.
  I like to eat this pie, warm or cold, with a crisp, well-dressed salad and new potatoes, ideally fresh from the garden, boiled and emulsified in melted butter.

CHICKEN PIE

This classic dish never fails to delight family or friends. Serve with hot seasonal vegetables.

Serves 6

EQUIPMENT
1 9in/23cm pie plate

INGREDIENTS
1 quantity rich shortcrust made with 12oz/350g flour (see page 89)
egg glaze

FOR THE FILLING
2oz/55g butter
1 large onion, finely chopped
1 carrot, julienned
1 stick celery, finely chopped
2 sprigs thyme
6 chicken breasts
4oz/115g mushrooms, sliced
pinch cayenne pepper
salt and pepper

FOR THE SAUCE
2oz/55g butter
1½ tbsp flour
½ pint/300ml milk
1 bay leaf, large pinch mace, powdered,
6 crushed peppercorns
¼-½ pint/150-300ml good chicken stock
small handful of fresh parsley, chopped
1-2 tbsp double cream
lemon juice
salt and pepper

1. PREPARING THE FILLING

Melt half the butter in a large frying pan and add the onion. Sauté gently until lightly golden, then add the carrot, celery and thyme. Stir-fry for a further 5 minutes. Season and transfer to a china plate.

Add the remaining butter to the pan and sauté the chicken in the hot fat until evenly browned all over. Remove with a slotted spoon, transfer to a china plate and cover loosely with kitchen foil. Quickly sauté the mushrooms in the remaining buttery juices and sprinkle over the cayenne pepper and seasoning. Remove with a slotted spoon and keep to one side.

2. PREPARING THE SAUCE

Melt the butter in a clean frying pan over a moderate heat. Stir in the flour and leave to bubble for 30 seconds, stirring frequently until the roux is the colour of pale straw. Remove from the heat and add some milk, stirring it in well to make a smooth paste. Add the bay leaf, mace and peppercorns. Transfer back to the heat, gradually adding the rest of the milk and stirring continually until the sauce has thickened. Stir in ¼ pint/150ml chicken stock and leave to simmer until the sauce has reduced to a smooth consistency. Add the cream and the parsley, and adjust the flavour with 1-2 squeezes of lemon juice and extra seasoning if required.

3. FILLING THE PIE

Slice each chicken breast down the centre and cut into thin discs. Stir into the sauce with the reserved onion and mushrooms. Leave uncovered, gently simmering over a low heat for 20 minutes. Stir occasionally and add more chicken stock if the sauce becomes too thick. Remove from the heat and transfer to a large, shallow china bowl to allow to cool.

Line the plate with one-third of the chilled pastry and add the cooled filling. Roll out half the remaining pastry for a lid and seal the edges with egg wash. Cut decorations for the pie lid from the remaining piece of pastry. Leave the completed pie in the fridge for 10-15 minutes to allow the pastry to firm, then paint over with egg wash before cooking in a preheated oven at 375°F/190°C/gas mark 5 for 30 minutes until the surface of the pie is a rich mid-gold colour.

PHEASANT AND CHESTNUT PIE

The natural sweetness of the chestnuts combines pleasantly with the game in this excellent rustic pie. When you buy chestnuts, look out for ones with smooth, shiny shells that feel heavy for their size. Chestnuts dehydrate as they age and become lighter.

Serves 4

EQUIPMENT
1 oblong pie dish, 11 × 7in/28 × 17.5cm and 2in/5cm deep

INGREDIENTS
1 brace of oven-ready pheasants
8oz/225g fresh chestnuts
1-2oz/25-55g butter
1 medium onion, finely chopped
1 level tbsp plain flour
1 pint/600ml hot chicken stock
1-1½ tbsp redcurrant jelly, to taste
juice of 1 small orange
rind of ½ orange, pared
1 tsp wine vinegar
salt and pepper
1 bay leaf
½ quantity puff pastry (see page 89)
egg wash

1. PREPARING THE PHEASANTS
Cut each pheasant into 4, removing any pieces of backbone. Clean and dry each portion, cutting away the yellowish fat that clings to some of the meat.

2. SHELLING THE CHESTNUTS
Score a cross on the side of each chestnut and drop them into boiling water for 2 minutes. Drain, peel away the shell and set to one side. If you use tinned chestnuts, drain them and add them to the casserole 5 minutes before the end of cooking.

3. PREPARING THE PIE FILLING
Melt the butter in a frying pan over low to moderate heat and cook the pheasant pieces until they are brown all over. Use a slotted spoon to transfer the pheasant to a casserole dish. Add the onion and sauté until light golden. Stir-fry the chestnuts with the onions for 2 minutes, then transfer to the casserole dish. Stir the flour into the residue in the frying pan. Stirring continually for 3-4 minutes, leave to bubble and turn pale brown before adding the stock. Bring to the boil and stir in the redcurrant jelly, orange juice, pared orange rind, wine vinegar and seasoning. Pour the contents of the pan over the pheasant and add the bay leaf. Cook covered in a preheated oven at 350°F/180°C/gas mark 4 for 1 hour, stirring once halfway through.

Transfer the pheasant pieces, onion and chestnuts to a china plate to cool. When it is cool enough to handle, cut and pull away the meat from the breast bones. Place the meat in the pie dish and reduce the stock in the pan so that it just covers the meat in the dish.

4. COVERING THE PIE
Thinly roll out two-thirds of the chilled pastry so that it is slightly larger than the pie dish. Cut off 4 strips from around the edges, moisten them with egg wash and press them over the lip of the dish. Wedge a pie funnel into the centre of the filling and lay over the rolled-out pastry, pressing it onto the egg-washed strips to seal. Leave to rest and chill in the fridge with the remaining piece of dough until the pastry is firm. Trim and decorate the edges. Roll out the remaining piece of pastry and the trimmings to make the decorative motifs. Egg wash the surface of each decoration and the pie lid. Chill briefly before baking in a preheated oven at 425°F/220°C/ gas mark 7 for 25 minutes.

RABBIT PIE

Rabbit is low in cholesterol, cheap to buy and delicious in casseroles, and it makes a really lovely rustic pie.

Serves 4

INGREDIENTS
2 rabbits, skinned, cleaned and jointed
3-4 strips of streaky bacon
1 tbsp seasoned flour
2oz/55g butter
1 tbsp cooking oil
1½ large onions, chopped
1 dstsp fresh thyme, chopped
1 tbsp fresh parsley, chopped
1 bay leaf
2 sticks celery, chopped
3 parsnips, sliced into 1in/2.5cm discs
1 small carrot, cut into small cubes
1 quantity pâté brisée made with 8oz/225g flour (see page 93)

FOR THE SAUCE
1oz/25g butter
1 level tbsp flour
¾ pint/450ml hot chicken stock
1-2 tbsp double cream
1 tsp wine vinegar
1 level tsp English mustard powder
salt
freshly ground pepper

1. PREPARING THE FILLING
Leave the rabbit joints in a bucket of salted water overnight to get rid of the blood or change the water repeatedly until it stays clean. Use the rabbit head and hind quarters for stock. Brown the bacon and rabbit joints, rolled in seasoned flour, in a large pan containing 2oz/55g butter and the oil. Drain and transfer with a slotted spoon to a casserole dish.

Stir-fry the onions in the hot fat until they are lightly brown, then drain and add to the rabbit meat with the herbs. Stir-fry the vegetables in the remaining hot oil for 3-4 minutes. Stir into the rest of the ingredients in the casserole.

2. MAKING THE SAUCE
Melt the butter over a moderate heat and stir in the flour to make a straw-coloured roux. Slowly add the hot stock, stirring continually until the sauce is smooth. Stir in the cream, wine vinegar, mustard and seasoning, then pour over the ingredients in the casserole dish. Cover the dish and cook in a preheated oven at 350°F/180°C/gas mark 4 for up to 1½ hours until the rabbit seems tender. The cooking time will depend on the age of the rabbit – young rabbit needs less time. Test the meat with a skewer or sharp-pointed knife.

3. COVERING THE PIE
Leave the cooked rabbit to cool, then remove the meat and set it inside the pie dish. Reduce the stock if necessary. Roll out the chilled dough and make a lid for the pie dish. Bake in a preheated oven at 350°F/180°C/gas mark 4 for 25 minutes.

Pressing and baking pastry around an animal decorating the lid of a china casserole or a large pâté tureen makes an inventive and unusual pie crust, which immediately informs your guests of the content. China tureens decorated with birds or animals can be used in the same way with the appropriate fillings, and the crust can be carefully pulled away from the china lid to accompany the served filling. Look out for decorative pâté tureens in France or in some good delicatessens. The bottom of the dish is usually deep enough to hold a substantial amount of meat.

SPOILS OF THE FIELD PIE

One of the advantages of these game pies was the thick, raised pastry case, which was sturdy enough for the pie to be transported on the large-scale movable feasts that accompanied the rich on their shooting parties. Farm workers were sent to the fields with simpler versions.

Makes 1 9½in/24cm pie

EQUIPMENT
1 9½in/24cm oval, hinged tin pie mould

INGREDIENTS
1 quantity hot water crust made with 1lb/445g flour (see page 91)
egg glaze

FOR THE FILLING
1 pheasant
4oz/115g loin pork fat, cubed
1lb/450g venison, roughly cut into cubes
4oz/115g back pork fat
1 medium onion, coarsely chopped
1 tsp grated orange rind
¼ pint/150ml brandy, madeira or port
1 heaped tbsp fresh parsley, chopped
5 juniper berries, crushed
1 rounded tsp salt, ½ tsp pepper
5 fat garlic cloves, crushed
1 large chicken breast, sliced into 4
3 pieces green (unsmoked) back bacon
5oz/140g good quality herb sausagemeat

FOR THE JELLIED STOCK
2lb/900g pork and pheasant bones
1 medium onion, 1 small stick celery,
1 carrot, all roughly chopped
bouquet garni, 5-6 peppercorns, ½ tsp
salt

1. PREPARING THE FILLING

The day before the pie is to be made remove the meat from the pheasant. Cut the breast meat into cubes and add to the cubed loin fat. Coarsely mince the boned leg meat of the pheasant with the venison, pork fat and onion. Mix with the cubed meat and add the ingredients for the filling – excluding the chicken breast, bacon and sausage meat – and leave overnight.

2. PREPARING THE STOCK

Put the ingredients in a saucepan, cover with cold water and bring to the boil. Remove the scum that forms on the surface and leave to simmer for 2 hours. Strain through a double thickness of butter muslin and boil the liquid down to a good ½ pint/ 300ml.

3. FILLING THE PIE

While the pastry is warm and malleable, roll it out, reserving one-third for the lid. Line the greased tin with the larger piece. Quickly and carefully press the pastry into the shape of the mould, pressing the seams well together so there are no cracks. Spoon the game mixture into the case until it is about one-third full. Add a layer of chicken and bacon, then another layer of game. Next add a layer of sausagemeat before adding the rest of the game mixture, which should be pressed into a shallow dome shape. Moisten the pastry around the edges and cover with the remaining piece for the lid. Make a hole in the centre and insert a small funnel made from a roll of kitchen foil. Decorate with leaves and bake a rose, a tassel or a circular coil separately to add to the pie to cover the hole in the centre through which the jelly will be poured. Paint over the pie lid with egg glaze and bake on a rigid baking tray in a preheated oven at 400°F/200°C/ gas mark 6 for 1 hour. Cover the pastry lid with a double thickness of kitchen foil and return to the oven to continue cooking at 350°F/180°C/gas mark 4 for a further hour. Leave to cool in the tin, but pour the jellied stock slowly into the pie through the funnel while the pie is still warm. Leave the pie to chill overnight.

PINK MARBLED FAN-SHAPED BISCUITS

*These pretty biscuits, with their delicate flavour and unusual marbled
appearance, will enhance the simplest plate of fresh summer fruits. When they
are served with hot poached fruits, warm the biscuits slightly in the oven.*

Makes approximately 28 biscuits

EQUIPMENT
*1 fan-shaped template cut from thin
card*

INGREDIENTS
*1 quantity pâté sucrée, made with
8oz/225g flour, an extra 1oz/25g of
caster sugar and an extra tsp of vanilla
essence (see page 92)
a few drops of red food colouring
egg wash*

1. MARBLING THE DOUGH
Remove the chilled dough from the
fridge and cut off about one-third.
Place the larger portion in a plastic
bag and return to the fridge. From the
smaller piece of dough take a small
piece, about the size of a walnut, and
colour it pale pink with the food
colouring. Knead it back into the
dough until the whole piece is evenly
coloured a soft pink.

Unwrap the uncoloured piece and
divide it into 2. Roll out the pink
piece of dough and the 2 uncoloured
pieces into thickish, oblong slabs.
Sandwich these together with egg
wash, with the coloured piece in the
centre, and press them together
lightly with a rolling pin.

2. CUTTING OUT THE BISCUITS
Use a sharp knife to cut through the
pastry slab to make slices ½in/12mm
wide. Keeping the remaining pastry
covered, thinly roll out one slice at a
time onto a lightly floured board or
marble slab. Use the template as a
guide to cut out 1 or 2 fan shapes.
Provided they are still moist, the
remaining pastry scraps can be
pressed together and re-rolled to
make another fan. Use the remaining
slices of pastry in the same way.

If you find cutting out the fan
shapes a little fiddly, use a simple
fluted or decorative biscuit cutter
instead.

3. DECORATING THE BISCUITS
Press a patterned piece of wood or any
small object with a strong pattern
that will impress into the pastry (see
page 19). Alternatively, use the blunt
side of the knife to make a criss-cross
pattern over the surface of the pastry.

4. COOKING THE BISCUITS
Transfer the pastry shapes to a lightly
greased baking sheet with a palette
knife and chill for 20 minutes in the
fridge. Cook in a preheated oven at
375°F/190°C/gas mark for 6 minutes.
Remove from the oven, leave to cool
slightly and lightly egg wash the
surface of each one. Return to the
oven for a further 2 minutes to give
the decorated side a shiny, glazed
surface.

Serve the biscuits with summer
fruits and thick, chilled cream or
crème fraîche. If you want to store
them for a short period, keep them in
an airtight tin; they may be frozen if
you want to keep them for longer.
Always crisp lightly in a moderate
oven before using.

AUTUMN TARTLETS WITH COUNTRY GARDEN FRUITS

Strongly veined garden leaves make excellent templates for pastry leaf decorations, and they can be used with these flavoured cream cheese tartlets.

Makes 8 tartlets

EQUIPMENT
8 small tartlet tins
leaf-shaped biscuit cutters in different shapes or 4-5 small garden leaves for templates
pastry piping bag fitted with a 6-star nozzle

INGREDIENTS
1 quantity pâté sucrée made with 8oz/225g flour (see page 92)
egg wash

FOR THE FILLING
4oz/115g rich cream cheese or curd cheese if you prefer
2 tbsp quince jelly or crabapple jelly or lemon curd
a small selection of country garden or hedgerow fruits, including some or all of crabapples (lightly poached to soften), damsons, blackberries, elderberries, plums and greengages
jam glaze

1. MAKING THE TARTLET CASES
Divide the chilled pastry into 2 and return one piece in a plastic bag to the fridge. Roll out the remaining piece and thinly line the greased tartlet tins. Chill again for 25 minutes. Fill with soft paper towel and baking beans and bake blind in a preheated oven at 400°F/200°C/gas mark 6 for 12 minutes or until the pastry is lightly golden. Remove the paper and beans and bake for a further 4-5 minutes until the cases are a mid-gold colour around the edges. Take care that they do not burn. Leave to cool slightly before turning out onto a wire cooling rack.

2. MAKING PASTRY LEAVES
Thinly roll out the remaining piece of dough and press differently shaped garden leaves firmly into the pastry to make a clear impression but taking care not to pierce the pastry. Cut around the outline with a sharp, small knife or a scalpel before carefully peeling away the leaf (see page 21). Alternatively, simply stamp out the leaves with a leaf-shaped biscuit cutter, using several different patterns and scoring them with a knife to simulate the veins. Place the pastry leaves in the fridge to chill thoroughly then lightly brush with egg wash. Transfer them to a baking tray and cook in a preheated oven at 400°F/200°C/gas mark 6 for 6-8 minutes until mid-gold at the edges. Leave to cool slightly before removing with a palette knife to a wire cooling rack.

3. MAKING THE FILLING
If you are using lemon curd mix it with the cream cheese. If you are using jelly melt it gently in a small saucepan, leave to cool but not solidify and beat into the cream cheese. Pipe the mixture into the tartlet shells. Carefully arrange the fruit over the filling and paint with warm jam glaze (see page 16). Add the pastry leaves, pressing the twig end of each one into the cream to secure it.

Eat the tartlets the day they are made if possible because the cream cheese filling will soften the pastry and make it soggy if they stand for too long.

PLUM PIE WITH MASCARPONE

*Sweetly acidic plums go perfectly with this more-ish pastry crust. The mild flavour
and smooth texture are quite different from shortcrust. Finish off the tart by lightly
sprinkling caster sugar over the lid to counteract the slight sharpness of the plums.*

Makes 1 9-9½in/23-24cm pie

EQUIPMENT
*1 round 9-9½in/23-24cm pie tin, 1in/
2.5cm deep and ideally with a small lip*

INGREDIENTS
*3oz/85g sugar
2 tbsp redcurrant jelly
2oz/55g butter
2 tbsp water
1¾-2lb/800-900g red plums; use other
plums or acid-tasting fruits if you
prefer or as available
½ tsp cinnamon, powdered
½ quantity mascarpone and soured
cream pastry made with 4½oz/125g
flour; cream cheese pastry may be used
instead if mascarpone is not available
egg glaze (see page 29)*

1. MAKING THE FILLING
Melt the sugar, redcurrant jelly and butter in a small saucepan with the water over a low heat. Set to one side. Pack the plums together in one layer over the base of the tin and sprinkle over the cinnamon. Pour over the warm, buttery redcurrant juices from the saucepan and place the tin in a preheated oven at 375°F/190°C/gas mark 5 for about 10 minutes, basting the plums several times. They should be barely tender but not soft so that they keep their shape later when they are cooked under the pastry crust. Leave the plums and syrup in the tin to cool.

2. COVERING THE PIE
Thinly roll out the pastry and cover the tin, placing moist strips of dough around the rim first. Trim off the excess pastry with a sharp knife, following the chilling and trimming instructions on page 94 to prevent shrinkage. Use a large pastry brush to glaze the lid evenly with egg wash and bake in a preheated oven at 375°F/ 190°C/gas mark 5 for 25 minutes until the pastry looks slightly golden and has an appetizing glaze.

Serve warm or cold with a side dish of chilled thick cream – and don't forget to warn your guests about the plum stones.

SQUIRREL TREAT PIE WITH AUTUMN LEAVES

The glorious shapes and colours of fallen leaves inspired the lid of this delicious creamy caramel nut pie, which is made with plain and chocolate pastry.

Makes 1 8in/20cm pie

EQUIPMENT
1 8in/20cm rounded, fluted, loose-bottomed tin, 1in/2.5cm deep

INGREDIENTS
1 quantity chocolate pastry made with 8oz/225g flour (see page 92)
½ quantity pâté sucrée made with 4oz/115g flour for the decorations (see page 92)
egg glaze

FOR THE CARAMEL SAUCE
2oz/50g pine nuts or skinned and roughly chopped hazelnuts
8oz/225g pecan nuts
6oz/175g walnuts
4oz/115g butter
11oz/300g granulated sugar
8fl oz/250ml double cream

1. LINING THE TIN
Divide the chilled chocolate pastry into 2 unequal pieces, wrapping the smaller piece in a plastic bag and returning it to the fridge. Use the larger piece to line the tin and return it to the fridge for at least 20 minutes.

2. PREPARING THE NUTS
If you are using hazelnuts place them on a tray under a hot grill for a few moments until they are lightly brown. Rub them briskly in a clean tea towel to remove the papery skins, then chop them roughly and mix them with the other nuts. Briefly re-heat in oven.

3. MAKING THE CARAMEL SAUCE
Slowly melt the butter in a thick-bottomed pan and add the sugar. Cook over a low to moderate heat, stirring continually. The sugar will turn a golden colour and form small, uneven clusters before it melts and caramelizes into a smooth sauce. As soon as the sugar has completely dissolved, stir in the cream. You should protect the hand that is holding the pan with a tea towel or something similar because the mixture will spit as you add the cream. The mixture will become lumpy and uneven, but keep stirring until it is smooth again.

Remove the caramel from the heat and immediately stir in the nuts, making sure they are evenly distributed through the mixture. Leave to cool, then carefully add to the lined tin. Roll out the smaller piece of chocolate pastry and cover the pie. Trim the edges neatly and return the pie to the fridge while you prepare the decoration.

4. DECORATING THE PIE
Roll out the chilled plain pâté sucrée and cut out leaf and nut decorations. Brush the surface of the pie with egg wash and press the lightly egg-washed motifs lightly in place. Chill and lightly glaze with egg wash again before cooking in a preheated oven at 375°F/190°C/gas mark 5 for 25 minutes. Do not leave it any longer or the pastry will burn. Serve warm with chilled crème fraîche.

APRICOT AND ALMOND PASTE PUFFS

Almond paste seems to have an especial affinity with apricots, and when the two are sealed and baked in a latticed case of puff pastry and finished off with caramelized icing sugar, the results are irresistible.

Makes 9 pastries

INGREDIENTS
1 quantity puff pastry made with 7oz/200g flour (see page 89)
egg glaze
9 fresh, ripe but firm apricots, stoned and halved
sifted icing sugar for glazing

FOR THE ALMOND PASTE
8oz/225g ground almonds
4oz/115g icing sugar, sifted
4oz/115g caster sugar
whites of 2 eggs
a few drops of pure almond essence (optional)

1. MAKING THE ALMOND PASTE
Combine the dry ingredients in a mixing bowl. Whisk the egg whites until they are just foamy and mix into the dry ingredients to form a soft, moist paste. Add almond essence if wished. Leave to become firm in the fridge. The paste can be made several days in advance and kept covered in the fridge.

2. PREPARING THE PUFF CASES
Divide the chilled pastry into 2 equal pieces and return one piece in a plastic bag to the fridge. Roll out the remaining piece into a square 13 × 13in/33 × 33cm. Divide the almond paste into 9 equal pieces and roll each piece in a little icing sugar in the palms of your hands to form a ball. Lightly press the paste to form circles about 3in/7.5cm across and place them evenly across the surface of the pastry, leaving 1in/2.5cm between each paste disc and between the discs and the edges of the pastry. Paint a little egg wash around each disc, then press 2 apricot halves, cut sides down and slightly overlapping, over the centre of the marzipan.
Roll out the second piece of chilled pastry into an oblong 13 × 14in/ 33 × 36cm. Use a lattice roller cutter to make a lattice pattern the full length of the longer side. Gently ease out the cuts to form the lattice pattern, then roll the pastry carefully around a rolling pin and transfer it over the top of the fruit and almond paste. Unroll the pastry carefully to drape it so that it covers the small mounds. Press around the circles with

your fingertips to seal the pastry.
Use a 3½in/9cm plain biscuit cutter to stamp out 9 pastries, keeping the apricots in the centre of the circles. Lightly coat the surface of each pastry with egg glaze before transferring them to a lightly greased baking tray. Set this tray on a hot baking sheet to ensure that the base of the pastries cook thoroughly, and bake the pastries in a preheated oven at 425°F/220°C/gas mark 7 for 15 minutes.

3. GLAZING THE PASTRIES
Transfer the pastries from the baking tray and arrange them evenly on a wire grilling rack. Dredge lightly with icing sugar so that the surface of the pastries is completely covered. Set them under a hot grill so that there is about 2in/5cm between the heat and the icing sugar. Keep watch as the icing sugar melts and caramelizes – it will take only 1-2 minutes. Don't worry if small scorch marks appear; these will not detract from the flavour. These puffs are undeniably more delicious when served warm with a little pouring cream.

CHOCOLATE AND GINGER PECAN TARTLETS

Line the tins and make the Neapolitan stripe pastry as thinly as possible to make the tartlets as light and delicate as you can because the filling is so rich. The pleasantly hot flavour of preserved stem ginger gives the rich chocolate sauce a warm, fiery taste.

Makes 4 tartlets

EQUIPMENT
4 4in/10cm tartlet tins, plain or fluted

INGREDIENTS
1 quantity rich shortcrust made with 8oz/225g flour (see page 89)
egg wash

FOR THE SYRUP
5oz/140g plain chocolate
4 eggs
3oz/85g butter, melted
8fl oz/250ml pure maple syrup
3-4 drops pure vanilla essence
4 1in/2.5cm pieces of stem ginger
8oz/225g pecan nuts, shelled

FOR THE CHOCOLATE PASTRY
1 tsp powdered drinking chocolate
$\frac{1}{2}$ tsp cocoa powder
$1\frac{1}{2}$ tsp caster sugar
2 drops pure vanilla essence

1. MAKING THE SYRUP
Melt the chocolate in a bowl over a pan of warm water taken from the heat. Whisk the eggs, butter, syrup and vanilla essence together, then stir into the melted chocolate with the chopped ginger. Pour half the chocolate syrup into a sauceboat, cover and reserve. Leave the remaining syrup in the pan, stir in the nuts and set to one side.

2. MAKING THE CHOCOLATE PASTRY
Cut 2 pieces from the pastry, each weighing about 3oz/85g. Knead the ingredients for the chocolate pastry into one of these until it is evenly combined. Return the pastry pieces, separately wrapped, to the fridge for 25 minutes.

3. LINING THE TARTLET TINS
Thinly roll out the largest piece of dough and line the tins. Combine any moist scraps with the 3oz/85g of plain dough. Place the lined tins in the fridge to firm the dough.

4. PREPARING THE NEAPOLITAN PASTRY
Roll out the chocolate pastry into a square 4 × 4in/10 × 10cm. Divide the remaining plain dough into 2 and roll them out into squares, 4 × 4in/10 × 10cm. Paint a light egg wash over the surface of one of the plain squares and press the square of chocolate dough over it. Paint that with egg wash and press the other plain square on the top, forming a sandwich with the chocolate dough in the centre. Lightly roll the pastry both ways to press the layers firmly together.

5. MAKING THE NEAPOLITAN STRIPS
Use a sharp knife to cut down into the pastry sandwich as you would slice a block of Neapolitan icecream to make 16 thin strips, each about $\frac{1}{8}$in/3mm wide. Turn the strips on their sides so that the 3 layers are exposed.

6. FILLING THE TARTLET CASES
Almost fill each of the pastry shells with pecan and chocolate syrup. Egg wash the edges of the tartlet cases and lay 4 of the pastry strips, criss-cross over each tartlet, pressing the ends down over the edges and removing the excess pastry with your thumb. Egg wash over the strips with a small brush and set the tartlets on a hot baking sheet to cook in a preheated oven at 375°F/190°C/gas mark 5 for about 25 minutes. Serve with the reserved syrup.

MARBLED TEA EGGS WITH PLUM SAUCE

Each year I serve these Chinese-style tea eggs in filo pastries with Christmas drinks.
They are a refreshing and delicious alternative to the endless mountain of sausage
rolls and mince pies – although do look at the alternative mince tart recipe on page 82.

Makes 24

EQUIPMENT
1 tin bun case with 12 impressions, each
2½in/6cm across

INGREDIENTS
6 sheets, approximately 9 × 9in/
23 × 23cm, of commercially made frozen
filo pastry, defrosted according to the
maker's instructions (see page 92)
egg wash or melted butter to glaze

FOR THE MARBLED EGGS
24 quails' eggs
1½ pints/900ml water

FOR THE TEA MIXTURE
1½ tbsp black tea, preferably Chinese
1 tbsp dark soy sauce
½ tsp salt
½ stick cinnamon
1 star anise

FOR THE DIPPING SAUCE
6 tbsp hoisin sauce
2 tbsp plum sauce

1. PREPARING THE FILO CASES

Cut out 48 squares, each measuring approximately 3 × 3in/7.5 × 7.5cm, from the filo, then stack the squares one on top of the other in a neat pile and cover with a damp cloth. Make the filo in two batches. First, lightly oil the impressions in the bun case with a little butter and press one filo square into each one. Use a small paintbrush to apply a little egg wash in the centre and over the edges of the squares, then press another square over the first in such a way that all 8 corners are visible and the cases look like small waterlilies. Lightly egg wash again and bake the cases in a preheated oven at 400°F/200°C/gas mark 6 for 3 minutes. Make and bake the remaining filo cases in the same way. Turn them out and set them to one side on a wire cooling rack.

2. PREPARING THE TEA EGGS

Add the water to a saucepan and bring to the boil. Use a spoon to lower the eggs carefully into the water, turn down the heat to a simmer and leave the eggs to cook for 2 minutes. Drain and leave to cool. Gently crack the shells all over with a teaspoon.

Add the ingredients of the tea mixture to the water in which you boiled the eggs and bring it back to the boil. Submerge the cracked eggs in the liquid and reduce the heat to a simmer. Leave the eggs to cook for about 15 minutes, remove the saucepan from the heat and allow the eggs to cool in the tea. Remove them from the cooled liquid and very carefully peel away the cracked shells. Quails' eggs have a tough skin beneath the shell, so cut through the shell with the point of a knife so that you can peel off the skin and shell together. When you have peeled the eggs you will find that the surface is covered in a cobweb pattern where the tea soaked through the cracks.

3. MAKING THE DIPPING SAUCE

Mix together the ingredients for the spicy plum sauce and add a small pool to each plate alongside two or more of the filo cases, each containing an egg. Sliced spring onions and crisp juliennes of cucumber together with a scarlet radiccio leaf would make a colourful garnish for this eye-catching festive treat.

ALTERNATIVE MINCE TARTS

These light and delicious tarts are a variation on the standard rich shortcrust mince tart. For best results use home-made mincemeat or a good quality bought one made with brandy or sherry and make your own marzipan.

Makes 24 tarts

EQUIPMENT
2 tin bun cases, each with 12 round impressions

INGREDIENTS
8 sheets, approximately 9 × 9in/ 23 × 23cm, of commercially made frozen filo pastry, defrosted according to the maker's instructions (see page 92) 12oz/350g mincemeat egg wash or melted butter to glaze

FOR THE ALMOND PASTE
4oz/115g finely ground almonds 2oz/55g icing sugar 2oz/55g caster sugar 1 white of egg, whisked until foamy

1. PREPARING THE ALMOND PASTE
This is best made at least a day in advance so that it can firm up a little. Mix all the ingredients together, press them into a moist ball and store, wrapped in a plastic bag, in the fridge.

2. MAKING THE FILO TARTS
Use a sharp knife to cut each sheet of pastry into 9 squares approximately 3 × 3in/7.5 × 7.5cm. Stack the squares into several small piles and cover with a damp teacloth to prevent them from drying out and becoming too brittle to work with.

Lightly grease the bun tins. Egg glaze 2 squares so that they adhere and place them centrally in one of the impressions, angled so that all 8 corners are visible and evenly spaced to form an 8-pointed star. Set to one side.

Press a square of pastry lightly into the cup of your hand and place into the centre of it 1 tsp of marzipan, lightly pressed into a disc 1in/2.5cm across. Spoon 1 level tsp of mincemeat over it. Lightly glaze the inside edges of the pastry with egg wash and wrap the square of pastry neatly around the filling. Resist the temptation to overfill, or it will seep out during cooking. Press the egg-glazed filled pastry, seam side down, into the centre of one of the filo cases. Repeat with the remaining pastry. Lightly egg wash the centres and bake in a preheated oven at 400°F/200°C/gas mark 6 for 4 minutes until golden around the edges. Leave to cool slightly before carefully turning out. Serve warm from the oven dusted with icing sugar; try adding dollops of chilled crème fraîche or mascarpone.

CHRISTMAS CRANBERRY PIE

*This large pie would be ideal for a Christmas party. Dust with icing sugar, using
a stencil to make a pretty Christmas motif for the top, and serve with chilled
pouring cream.*

*Makes 1 11-12in/28-30cm tart; the
quantities given make enough for 12
people, but if you want to make a
smaller tart, make the pastry with
8oz/225g flour and halve the ingredients
for the filling*

EQUIPMENT
*1 11-12in/28-30cm fluted flan tin,
1½in/4cm deep or oblong tin
9in/23cm × 12in/30cm*

INGREDIENTS
*1 quantity orange and cardamon pastry
made with 1lb/450g flour (see page 94)
egg glaze*

FOR THE FILLING
*2½lb/1.1kg fresh cranberries, or use
defrosted frozen cranberries
8 tbsp redcurrant jelly
10 tbsp caster sugar
8 tbsp water
2oz/55g butter*

1. PREPARING THE FILLING
Place the cranberries in a large,
shallow dish with the redcurrant jelly,
sugar and water and dot over with the
butter. Place in a preheated oven at
375°F/190°C/gas mark 5 for 8 minutes
until the juices start to run. Baste
twice to amalgamate the ingredients,
then remove from the oven and leave
the fruit to cool in the syrup.

2. PREPARING THE PASTRY CASE
Divide the chilled pastry into 2 pieces,
returning one piece, wrapped in a
plastic bag to the fridge. Use the other
piece to line the flan tin. Place the
lined tin in the fridge to allow the
pastry to firm.

3. FILLING THE CASE
Strain the cranberry juice into a
saucepan and heat until reduced by
half and thickened into a rich syrup.
Pour the warm syrup back over the
fruit. If you leave it for too long it
begins to solidify, but if this happens
scrape the jelly over the fruit and stir
it in. Spoon the cooled fruit into the
pastry shell and egg glaze the edge.
Roll our the remaining pastry and
cover the fruit. Trim the edges of the

pastry and paint the surface of the
tart with egg wash. Bake in a
preheated oven at 375°F/190°C/gas
mark 5 for 25-30 minutes. Leave to
cool before sieving icing sugar over
the top of the still warm pastry.

SALT DOUGH SHEAF

Attractive wall and windowsill decoration can be made to look as realistic and intricate or as simple and naïve as you wish. The pastry decorations last indefinitely, but the dry, crisp texture does become a little fragile with age.

Makes 4 6in/15cm shapes or 2 12in/30cm shapes

INGREDIENTS
4 cups plain flour
2 cups salt
1 tsp cooking oil
water to mix
1 egg white, lightly beaten for glazing

1. MAKING THE DOUGH
Add the flour, salt and oil to a mixing bowl, then slowly pour in water in a thin stream, combining the ingredients with one hand, until you have a stiff dough. Press and knead the paste very lightly on a floured board, but take care not to fold and trap air inside the dough because this will cause unwanted air bubbles to form during cooking.

2. SHAPING THE DOUGH
Grease and lightly flour a baking sheet, then make the decorative shapes straight onto the sheet. If you try to transfer intricate or delicate shapes to the baking sheet after they are formed you may damage them. Follow the design shown in the illustration or make your own. This kind of pastry can be cut with biscuit cutters or formed into shapes in large or small moulds, and it holds its shape beautifully while it dries out in the oven. Lightly glaze the shapes, which should be cooked at a very low temperature – 250°F/120°C/gas mark $\frac{1}{2}$ – for, depending on their size, 2 hours or more. The best way to tell when the pastry is ready is when it feels crisp and dry and has a golden colour.

These are ideal projects for play groups, where small children will find particular pleasure in making their own artistic renditions of animals, castles, nursery rhyme characters and other imaginary shapes.

HOW TO MAKE THE PASTRIES
USED IN THIS BOOK

RICH SHORTCRUST

A few simple rules must be observed if you are to achieve perfect shortcrust pastry. A light hand and cool fingertips are required so that you can lightly and quickly knead the ingredients together. Heavy kneading and over-handling the dough will develop the gluten, the protein in the flour, which is formed when you add water to it. If this is over-worked, it becomes more elastic and produces a tough pastry.

Pastry made from 12oz/350g flour is required for large covered and decorated pies. Substitute 1oz/25g lard for the same amount of butter to make a crisper, shorter pastry. Use all butter if you want the pastry decorations to keep their shape well during cooking.

INGREDIENTS
8oz/225g plain flour
pinch of salt
5oz/140g butter
1 egg yolk from a medium egg, whisked with 1-2 tbsp cold water
or
12oz/350g plain flour
pinch of salt

8oz/225g butter
1 egg yolk from a large egg, whisked with 2-2$\frac{1}{2}$ tbsp cold water

Sieve the flour and salt into a mixing bowl. Remove the butter from the fridge and, using 2 knives, chop it into small pieces into the flour. Rub the mixture, quickly and lightly, with your fingertips until it resembles fine breadcrumbs. Use a palette knife to mix enough of the egg and water mix into the crumbs until they begin to cling together. Then press them lightly together to form a soft, moist, but not sticky dough. Knead the dough lightly on a floured board for 4-5 seconds to smooth out any cracks, then wrap it in a piece of soft kitchen paper and place it in plastic bag. Leave to chill and rest in the fridge for 25 minutes before using.

Cheese Pastry

Add 4oz/115g of grated dry, mature cheddar cheese into the breadcrumb-like mixture together with a pinch of cayenne pepper and dry mustard before you add the egg and water mixture.

Green Pastry

Add a large handful of a mixture of one-third fresh spinach leaves to two-thirds finely chopped green herbs, including parsley, thyme and marjoram.

PUFF PASTRY

Because all the ingredients for puff pastry, or *pâté feuilletée*, have to be kept chilled, even to the point of using iced water, one of the best pieces of advice that can be offered is never to make it on a hot day or when the kitchen is warm from other cooking. The whole operation could be ruined if the butter is allowed to become too soft.

Although decorative motifs puff up, they keep their shapes quite well, and they can be used to make wonderfully ornate, rich golden crusts that have a deliciously buttery aroma. For a change, you can add chilled cream instead of water to the basic dough to make a particularly delicate pastry.

This quantity will make enough for a top crust for a pie for 8 people. To save time and improve the quality of the pastry, double up on the quantities so that you can freeze portions for future use.

7oz/200g strong white flour
½ tsp salt
7oz/200g butter, chilled
5 tbsp iced water, including 1 tsp lemon juice

Sift the flour and salt into a mixing bowl and add about a quarter of the butter, cutting it roughly into the flour with 2 knives. Return the remaining butter to the fridge. Mix the flour, salt and butter with your fingertips until it resembles fine breadcrumbs, then mix to a firm but moist dough (*détrempe*) with the cold water and lemon juice. Wrap in a plastic bag and chill for 30 minutes.

   Place the remaining butter between two pieces of non-stick kitchen parchment and pound it, pressing it into a square about 3½ × 3½in/9 × 9cm and about ¾in/2cm deep. At this stage the butter must not be too soft or too hard. Ideally, it should be a similar texture to the dough so that they can be more easily rolled out together.

   Unwrap the dough and roll it into a square about 6½ × 6½in/16.5 × 16.5cm and place the butter diagonally over the centre of the pastry. Pull up the four corners of the dough to cover the butter – it will look like the back of a square envelope – and use a rolling pin to press down the seams

to seal them. Replace the dough in a plastic bag and return to the fridge to rest for 20 minutes. Remove the dough from the fridge and place it on a floured board, seam-side up.

1. Roll out the dough to a rectangle, 3 times as long as it is wide, always rolling away from you and not from side to side. Keep the edges and corners square, gently easing them out with your fingertips if necessary. Fold the top one-third down and the bottom one-third up to make 3 layers. Use a rolling pin to press the edges and seams gently together, then turn the dough 90 degrees to your right so that it would 'open' like a book. This is a turn.

2. Roll out once more into a rectangle 3 times as long as it is wide (it will probably be about 18 × 6in/ 45 × 15cm), fold the top one-third down and the bottom one-third up and use a rolling pin to press the edges and seams gently together, and turn 90 degrees as before.

3. Wrap and chill for 30 minutes.

Repeat steps 1, 2 and 3 twice more, including the chilling each time. One way of keep count of the number of turns is to mark the surface of the dough with the appropriate number of fingerprints before each chilling period.

The dough is now ready to use. If you are not going to use it immediately, wrap it in kitchen towel, cover it tightly in a plastic bag and leave it in the fridge for 2-3 days. Well wrapped, it will freeze beautifully The pastry takes about 1 hours to defrost at room temperature, but it is better to defrost it slowly in the fridge overnight.

FLAKY PASTRY
I think it would be fair to describe this crisp, buttery pastry as a traditional farmhouse pastry. It is the kind of pastry found covering a variety of both sweet and savoury pies arrayed over the solid-fuel cooker in a rural kitchen, fragrant with the scents of a good day's baking.

   Flaky pastry is similar to puff pastry but not as fine or layered. It is, though, quicker to make and is ideal for family meals during the week. The pastry is baked at the same temperature, and the small pieces of fat daubed between the layers of dough help to separate the flakes during cooking.

8oz/225g strong white flour
½ tsp salt
6oz/175g firm butter
5 tbsp cold water
1 tsp lemon juice

Sift the flour and salt into a mixing bowl. Divide the butter into 4 portions and cut one portion into the flour. Lightly rub it in with your fingertips, lifting the mixture frequently to aerate it, until it resembles fine breadcrumbs. Add the water the lemon juice and lightly mix together with a palette knife to make a firm, moist dough. Knead lightly to make it smooth and roll it into a strip 3 times as long as it is wide and about ¼in/5mm deep.

Use a pointed knife to add the next portion of butter, not too close to the edges of the dough, to cover two-thirds of the pastry, leaving the bottom one-third free of butter. Fold the bottom section over the middle and the top section, which is dotted with butter, over the middle so that the pastry is folded into 3 layers. Turn the pastry through 90 degrees so that an open end is towards you. Place the pastry in a plastic bag and leave it to chill in the fridge, together with the remaining 2 portions of butter, for 15-20 minutes.

Press the edges together with a rolling pin, then roll out the chilled pastry again. Repeat the same rolling, folding and sealing procedures with the third and fourth portions of butter, allowing the same chilling periods between each. Allow the pastry to chill for 1 hour before rolling out. Be careful not to roll it too thinly or you may press the layers of fat together, and prevent the flaky texture from forming.

HOT WATER CRUST

Because it contains only lard, hot water crust tastes rather bland. However, the taste can be greatly improved if 2oz/55g butter is used instead of the same amount of lard, even though this will soften the texture of the pastry and make it unsuitable for the large game pies that are a little tricky to demould without cracking. However, it is useful for smaller pies, which can be raised around the base of 1lb/450g jam jars or small wooden pie moulds

1lb/445g strong plain flour
1 tsp salt
6oz/175g lard, chopped
7fl oz/200ml mixed milk and water in equal amounts

Place the flour and salt in a bowl and make a well in the centre. Melt the lard in the milk and water and bring to the boil over medium heat. As soon as the mixture has boiled, pour it into the flour and stir vigorously until the ingredients are well mixed. When the dough has cooled a little, knead it until it is smooth, then place it in a bowl and cover it with a cloth. Leave for 15 minutes until the dough feels firmer and use immediately.

LIGHT WHOLEMEAL PASTRY

If you dislike wholemeal pastry because you find it too heavy in terms of both texture and taste, try this recipe, in which a mixture of plain white and wholemeal flours and a small amount of lard make a much lighter dough. This pastry keeps its shape well during cooking, which makes it ideal for decorative crusts.

The curry powder adds a subtle spicy flavour, but it should, of course, be omitted if the pastry is made for sweet pies and flans, when 1½oz/45g caster sugar should be used instead.

4oz/100g wholemeal flour, sifted
4oz/100g plain flour, sifted
pinch of salt
½ tsp mild curry powder
4oz/100g butter
1oz/25g lard or use 1oz/25g extra butter
1 egg yolk
approximately 2 tbsp water

Sift the flours, salt and curry powder into a mixing bowl and chop the fat into the ingredients with 2 knives. Combine with your fingertips to form a fine, breadcrumb-like consistency. Mix the egg yolk with water and stir into the mixture, quickly and lightly, with a palette knife. Press together into a soft, moist dough with floured hands. Knead lightly on a floured working surface to form a ball before wrapping it in soft kitchen towel in a plastic bag. Place it in the fridge for 25 minutes before use.

FILO (PHYLLO) PASTRY

Although home-made filo pastry is simplicity itself to make, the chief difficulty lies in rolling out the dough until it is almost transparent. I have suggested using shop-bought frozen filo pastry in the recipes in this book because they require a lot of neat cutting into small shapes, and frankly, the texture of the frozen pastry is easier to deal with.

I would, however, certainly use a home-made filo for an apple strudel or any similar recipe for which large sheets of pastry are required. In those circumstances the odd tear will enhance rather than detract from the appearance of the finished pastry.

10oz/285g plain all-purpose flour
pinch of salt
1 medium egg
approximately 6fl oz/200ml water
1 tsp sunflower oil

Sift the flour and salt into a bowl. Beat the egg and mix it with the water and oil. Work the liquid into the flour with a palette knife, then combine the mixture with one hand into a soft dough. Knead or beat the dough until it is smooth and elastic. Sprinkle the inside of a bowl with flour and place the dough inside. Cover and leave in a warm place for 20 minutes. Then leave the pastry to stand at room temperature for 5 minutes. The pastry is ready to use.

HERB PASTRY

This unusual pastry uses a delicate mixture of tender green herbs to enhance the basic rich shortcrust.

5oz/140g butter
8oz/225g plain flour, sifted
pinch of salt
1 dstsp fresh thyme, chopped
4-5 freshly torn basil leaves
1 dstsp marjoram, finely chopped
small handful parsley, finely chopped
2-3 chives, finely chopped
1 egg yolk mixed with 1-2 tbsp water

Knead the butter into the flour and salt until the mixture resembles fine breadcrumbs. Sprinkle over the chopped herbs and mix in the egg and water. Press into a soft dough, then knead lightly on a floured board to get rid of the cracks. Form the pastry into a ball and leave in a plastic bag, in the fridge for 30 minutes.

PÂTÉ SUCRÉE

This pastry, which is also known as French flan pastry, can be kept for up to 3 days if it is wrapped in soft kitchen towel and kept in a plastic bag in the fridge. For moulding or decorative work it is better to use freshly made, chilled pâté sucrée. Alternatively, press small pieces of dough into moulds or roll out the dough and line the tins in which you are going to cook it, then freeze them, wrapped in freezer bags. Defrost in the fridge. Cut or moulded decorations hold their shape better if the pastry is well chilled before cooking. Baked pastry shells can be frozen, although they are best lightly baked to recrisp them before use.

Cook pâté sucrée to biscuit stage, but do not let it over-cook because it burns quickly as it contains a high proportion of sugar. The pastry goes a little soggy if it is filled too far in advance, so if possible prepare it with the filling on the day you need it.

8oz/225g plain flour
4oz/115g butter, cut into small pieces
3½oz/90g caster sugar
large pinch salt
1-1¼ tsp vanilla essence
3 medium egg yolks

Sift the flour onto a board or marble slab. Make an open well in the centre and into it place the butter, sugar, salt, vanilla essence and egg yolks. Draw the fingertips of one hand together and, lightly and quickly, work the ingredients in the well with a bird-like, pecking motion until the mixture resembles scrambled eggs. Gradually draw in the flour and, using the same finger movement, quickly combine the remaining ingredients to form a crumb-like mixture. Gather together and lightly press the moist crumbs into a soft ball. Lightly knead the dough by pushing it away from you with the heel of your hand and drawing it back 4-5 times until the pastry is smooth. Wrap in paper towel and place in a plastic bag; chill for 1 hour. Knead before using.

PÂTÉ BRISÉE

This is made in the same way as pâte sucrée, but it is not sweetened. It is ideal for both sweet and savoury flans and tartlets, keeping its shape well during cooking. It should be used instead of shortcrust for a neater shaped tartlet.

8oz/225g plain flour
4oz/115g butter, lightly pounded until softened
2 egg yolks
1 level tsp salt
3½-4 tbsp cold water

Sift the flour onto a board or marble slab and make a large well in the centre. Place the butter, egg yolks and salt inside with most of the water and work together with the fingertips in a pecking motion as for pâté sucrée until the ingredients are partly mixed. Gradually work the flour into the mixture, still using your fingertip to pull the mixture into large crumbs. If the crumbs seem a little dry, sprinkle over more of the water. Press the dough together to form a soft, pliable dough that is not sticky. Work the dough onto a very lightly floured surface by pushing it away from you with the heel of your hand, drawing it back until it is smooth. Press the dough into a ball, wrap in a plastic bag and place in the fridge for at least 30 minutes.

The dough can be tightly wrapped in soft kitchen towel and a plastic bag and stored for up to 3 days in a fridge or for longer in a freezer. It is sometimes more convenient and time-saving to line tins with the rolled-out dough and freeze them in this state. Defrost in the fridge.

CHOUX PASTRY

Choux is one of the easiest pastries to make – follow the simple instructions properly and you can't go wrong.

Eggs make the pastry light, so incorporate as much egg as possible into the mixture until the dough is soft but still stiff enough to hold its shape. Also, make sure that you beat each egg in thoroughly before adding the next. Piped shapes will puff up to double their size when baked.

Fill choux pastries no more than 1 hour ahead or they become soggy. They can lose their pleasant crispness quite quickly even when they are left for some time unfilled. Place the pastries briefly in a moderate to high oven regain their crispness. Choux pastries are always best freshly made, but they will keep for a day or two in an airtight container. Recrisp in the oven.

5oz/140g plain flour
½ pint/300ml water
½ tsp salt
3½oz/90g butter
4 eggs

Fold a square of greaseproof paper down the centre and sift onto it the flour. Leave it to one side. Gently heat the water, salt and butter together in a moderate sized saucepan until the butter has melted. Turn up the heat and bring the contents of the pan to a rolling boil; remove from the heat. Shoot the flour from the paper into the liquid. Make sure you add all the flour at once or it will cook in small lumps. Immediately beat vigorously with a spatula for 4-5 seconds until the mixture is smooth and pulls away from the sides of the saucepan to form a soft ball in the centre. Return the pan to a low heat for a minute to evaporate some of the water and dry out the mixture. Tip the paste into a mixing bowl. Break 1 egg into a small bowl, beat it and set it to one side. Add the remaining eggs to the mixture, one by one, beating thoroughly between each addition, until the mixture looks well combined and smooth. Finally, beat in just enough of the reserved egg to make a dropping consistency that is soft and glossy but that holds its shape.

If you do not wish to use it

straight away, smear the warm surface with butter to prevent a crust from forming and leave, for several hours if necessary.

Using a pastry bag fitted with a ½in/12mm tube, pipe into shapes on greased and lightly floured baking sheets. Bake at 400°F/200°C/gas mark 6 for 25 minutes until crisp and pale brown. For sweet choux fill cooled pastries with sweet flavoured creams; for savoury choux use cream cheese or savoury fillings.

MASCARPONE AND SOURED CREAM PASTRY

Mascarpone is a delicately flavoured cow's milk cheese, which looks like a pale buttermilk-coloured whipped cream. It can be bought from most good delicatessens and the cheese counters of larger supermarkets. Should it be unavailable, use the cream cheese pastry recipe, which has a slightly stronger flavour but still tastes exceedingly good.

6oz/175g butter, softened
3 tbsp mascarpone soft cream cheese
3 tbsp soured cream
9oz/255g plain flour
pinch of salt

Place the butter, cream cheese and soured cream in a mixing bowl and beat them together. Mix in the sifted flour and salt with a palette knife. Finish off lightly with your fingertips

to make a soft, moist dough. Leave to chill for 45-60 minutes.

RICH CREAM CHEESE PASTRY

6oz/175g butter, softened
4 tbsp rich cream cheese
2 tbsp soured cream
8oz/225g plain flour
pinch of salt

Follow the method for Mascarpone and Soured Cream Pastry.

ORANGE AND CARDAMON PASTRY

8oz/225g plain flour
pinch of salt
8 green cardamom pods
4oz/115g butter, cut into small pieces
3½oz/90g caster sugar
3 egg yolks
grated zest of 1 orange

Sift the flour and salt onto a board and make an open well in the centre. Crush the cardamom pods by pressing them to release the small black seeds. Place the seeds in the corner of a small plastic bag and crush them with a rolling pin to make a fine powder. Shake the powdered seeds through a sieve and sprinkle them over the circle of flour. Place the butter, sugar, egg yolks and orange zest in the well. With the

fingers of one hand held together, work lightly and quickly until the mixture resembles scrambled eggs. Draw the flour into the mixture until it forms large, moist crumbs. Press them into a ball. Knead for 4-5 seconds until smooth, then wrap in a plastic bag and chill for 45 minutes.

CHOCOLATE PASTRY

This is ideal for making flans and tartlets for chocolate- and caramel-based cream fillings and biscuits.

8oz/225g plain flour
1 level tbsp cocoa powder
1 level tbsp drinking chocolate powder
4oz/115g butter, cut into small pieces
3oz/75g caster sugar
large pinch salt
3 egg yolks
1 tsp pure vanilla essence

Sift the dry ingredients onto a board. Make a well in the centre and add the butter, sugar, salt, eggs and vanilla essence. Draw the fingertips of one hand together and quickly and lightly work the ingredients in the well together until the mixture resembles scrambled eggs. Combine with the remaining ingredients until the mixture forms large, moist crumbs. Press them lightly together to form a soft ball. Knead the dough until it is smooth and free of cracks. Wrap it in soft tissue, place in a plastic bag and leave in the fridge to rest for 1 hour.

CREDITS AND ACKNOWLEDGEMENTS

I would like to thank the following for their generous help in loaning me some very beautiful props for photography, particularly Josephine Marston, who generously allowed me to use her beautiful home as an instant props house. Thanks also to Richard Scott Antiques, 30 High Street, Holt, Norfolk NR25 6BH, and to James and Caroline Layte, Humbleyard Fine Art, Waterfall Cottage, Swanton Morley, Norfolk, for exquisite china and furniture.

Other antiques were loaned by St Michael Plea, Bank Plain, Norwich; Holt Antique Centre, Albert Street, Holt, Norfolk; and Salhouse Hall Antiques, Salhouse, Norfolk.

For the loan of their gardens for photographic locations Victoria and Alan Cole, Benella, Swanton Morley, Norfolk; and Robin and Judy Don of Elmhan Wines, North Elmhan, Norfolk.

For kitchen equipment David Mellor, 4 Sloane Square, London SW1V 8EE.

For beautiful papers and fine paper decorations Paperchase, 213 Tottenham Court Road, London W1P 9AF; and The Italian Paper Shop, 11 Brompton Arcade, Knightsbridge, London SW3. For fabrics and wallpapers, Osborne and Little, 304–308 Kings Road, London SW3.

Food and other supplies John Blackburne, Norfolk Nutbrown Mushrooms, Cockley Cley Estate, near Swaffham, Norfolk; E.D. Broady, Family Butcher and Game Dealer, Swanton Morley, Norfolk; Connie Carne, my neighbour (for country garden flowers); Brian and Rosemary Clifton-Sprigg, Norfolk Herbs, Blackberry Farm, Dillington, Dereham, Norfolk; Bob Flowerdew, organic gardener *extraordinaire* (for garden fruits), Dickleborough, Norfolk; Trevor Pratt, Wet Fish Shop and Game Dealer, Unit 3 Nunn's Way, Dereham, Norfolk; and Redford Family Butcher and Delicatessen, 4 Norwich Street, Dereham, Norfolk.

Other thanks to Georgina Holloway from the Flour Advisory Bureau, 21 Arlington Street, London SW1A 1RN; and to Matthew Hardy, presently lecturing at the Cordon Bleu Cookery School, 114 Marylebone Lane, London W1M 6HH.

I would like to express special thanks to the editorial and design team at Cassell, who made this work both possible and enjoyable, and to my husband, Terry Pastor, for his assistance and unfailing support during the photographic sessions. Finally, thanks to Richard and Jenita Nemar-Smith at Reflections Professional Colour Laboratory, 4 Beckham Place, Edward Street, Norwich NR3 3DZ, for processing the films so efficiently and for their invaluable help and advice throughout.

INDEX